The Mystery of Divine Love

Fr. Wojciech Giertych, O.P.

The Mystery of Divine Love

EWTN Publishing, Inc.

Irondale, Alabama

EWTN Publishing, Inc.
5817 Old Leeds Road, Irondale, AL 35210

Distributed by Sophia Institute Press, Box 5284, Manchester, NH 03108.

paperback ISBN 978-1-68278-275-0
ebook ISBN 978-1-68278-276-7
Library of Congress Control Number: 2022938232

First printing

Contents

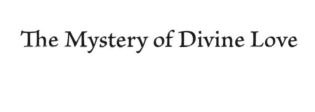

The Mystery of Divine Love

Foreword

Toward God, we need to be straightforward.

Unfortunately, we are often complicated. We think that we have to be pure and sinless to be able to approach God. We have our own ideas about ourselves, our world, and our Church and we would like to impose them upon God. We have our life's history with its ups and downs, with various experiences, some of them pleasant and others painful | — | all this hangs in our psyche, memory, and spiritual life and impacts our human encounters. Other people do not understand us, or they have other priorities, and this makes us uncomfortable.

As a result, we often hide behind a mask. Children are not like this. They are simple and direct in their relationships. They do not think that they have to merit trust and so they are immediately confident. They are not paralyzed by their blunders, because they know that they are loved. But we adults have learned how to manage ourselves, and so we often put on a mask that partly hides our face, hides our true self. Maybe we have committed some misdemeanours. Maybe we think that our cultural background or schooling was not up to standard and something better is expected of us. Such hiding may be an emotional distance, a constant turning to academic discourses or a superficial wittiness. Then the true self is never shown, and what is worse, it is never presented to God. Basically, this difficulty is not psychological but spiritual.

Toward God, we have to be like children. Of course, we need to be adult and responsible in the face of worldly challenges. This is understandable and normal. But before the face of God, we need to maintain a childlike simplicity and trust that we are in the hands of the loving Eternal Father. In the past we have committed shameful sins. We are worried about this and that. We have projects for our future. But all these concerns are not the most important and should not tarnish our encounter with God. If we relate to Him with childlike openness because Jesus has already redeemed us with His Gift of Self; if we locate our deepest hope within the mysterious divine Providence; and if we try to love God, even poorly, but truly, with our meagre little gifts given to Him, we immediately open up divine graces. This is fundamental and liberating.

We should not be bothered by the fact that we shall most likely not be known saints. We are who we are, with our own life and its joys and sufferings. Trusting that we are in God's hands, we surrender to Him like a child that grabs the hand of a parent while crossing a busy road. This then gives us confidence and allows us to bring the love of God into the commonplace situations in which we spend most of our time.

These homilies and conferences were preached in July 2016 during a weekend retreat for a group of laywomen in the guest house of the Sisters of Life in Stanford, New York. The participants recorded them and then asked that they be published. They retain an oral character and are not encumbered by footnotes. Obviously, as I preached, I shared the wisdom of many works that I had previously read. This is normal. We all do this, as we preach. We do not try to be original. We transmit received truths that ultimately originate in the Word of God. Hopefully these conferences will serve those who try to live more deeply with God.

Fr. Wojciech Giertych O.P.
Theologian of the Papal Household

Faith in the Risen Lord

"Many of the Jews had come to Martha and Mary to comfort them about their brother Lazarus, who had died. When Martha heard that Jesus was coming, she went to meet Him. But Mary sat at home. Martha said to Jesus, 'Lord, if You had been here, my brother would not have died. But even now, I know that whatever You ask of God, God will give You.' Jesus said to her, 'Your brother will rise.'

Martha said to Him, 'I know he will rise. In the resurrection on the last day.' Jesus told her, 'I am the Resurrection and the Life. Whoever believes in Me, even if he dies, will live. And whoever lives and believes in Me will never die. Do you believe this?' She said to Him, 'Yes, Lord. I have come to believe that You are the Christ. The Son of God. The One who is coming into the world.'"

—John 11:19–27

Martha, like Peter, declared her belief in Jesus. But shortly afterward, if we follow up reading the Gospel of St. John when Jesus said, "Open the tomb," Martha says, "No, no. It's four days since his funeral. The body is decomposing. There'll be a stench." And yet she said that she believes that Christ is the Son of God. She heard the words, "I am the Resurrection and the Life." We see here that also St. Peter recognized that Jesus is the Messiah. And yet when he is told He will die on the Cross, he says, "No, no! Not that."

So, just a declaration of faith is not yet sufficient. Faith has to seep into life, into all our reactions. Because faith opens us to grace, which heals. And it is sometimes difficult to develop a deeper faith.

St. Augustine once made a comment that in the Gospels there are three moments when Jesus raised someone from the dead. Jesus raised the daughter of Jairus, who was a little girl lying in bed; Jesus raised from the dead a young man from Nain, who was being carried to the cemetery; and Jesus raised from the dead Lazarus, who was already in the tomb for four days. St. Augustine compares this to three types of sin: sins that have just happened; sins that lead to permanent death in the soul, the death of the supernatural life; and sins that cause decomposition and stench. Jesus has the power to save us from all types of sin and to lead us to life everlasting. This is what we believe, and this is what we try to express in our faith, in our prayer, that we place our total hope in Him.

Prayer as an Exercise in Faith

"There was a woman afflicted with hemorrhages for twelve years. She suffered greatly at the hands of many doctors and had spent all that she had, yet she was not helped but only grew worse. She had heard about Jesus and came up behind Him in a crowd and touched His cloak. She said 'If I but touch His clothes, I shall be cured.' Immediately, her flow of blood dried up. She felt in her body that she was healed of her affliction.

Jesus, aware at once that power had gone out from Him, turned around in the crowd and asked: 'Who has touched My clothes?' But the disciples said to Him: 'You see how the crowd is pressing upon You and yet You ask, "Who touched Me?"' And He looked around to see who had done it. The woman, realizing what had happened to her, approached in fear and trembling. She fell down before Jesus and told Him the whole truth. He said to her: 'Daughter, your faith has saved you. Go in peace and be cured of your affliction.'

— Mark 5:25–34

The Gospel of St. Mark is basically the Gospel of St. Peter. Mark was a disciple of Peter, so the Gospel of Mark recalls the experiences and memories of Peter. Peter knew the country life in Capernaum, where people knew one another and where they came to see Jesus with their problems. Peter knew these people. And this woman must have been known in this small village. Everybody must have known that she was suffering, and she spent a lot of money on doctors. St. Luke, who was a doctor, recalls the same story. He mentions that she spent money on doctors, but he doesn't say that she suffered from them. Luke was careful not to question the reputation of doctors!

According to Jewish understanding, she was ritually unclean, so she was excluded from the community. She wasn't allowed to touch anybody. She had the courage to go beyond the rules, and she approached Jesus and touched the hem of Jesus' cloak with her finger, but with her faith, she touched Jesus' heart. And immediately aware that power had gone out of Him, Jesus turned around and said, "Who touched My clothes?" The disciples were surprised. Jesus was in a crowd, and everybody was pushing. So, what was the problem? Somebody touched Jesus. But the faith of this woman triggered the effusion of divine power, and Jesus noticed this. The exercised faith sparked something that Jesus experienced: the effusion of divine grace which passes through the glorified humanity of Jesus. Jesus could only make miracles when He met with a faith which was exercised.

In this story, we have the essence of contemplative prayer. It teaches us about prayer. Contemplative prayer is the exercise of faith. We can make a distinction between vocal prayer, when we have written text that we recite, and meditation, where we take a scene from the Gospel and we reflect upon it, we think about it, we try to pray around it, and if somebody asks us, "What did you meditate about?" we can speak about the subject matter. If we priests have to preach and meditate upon the text, we can find meaning in the text to preach about. But contemplative prayer is basically the exercise of faith, so there's not much content to recall. It is about the fact that I believe: "Jesus, You are here." And in this exercise of faith, our faith touches Jesus. There is a contact with Jesus.

Faith is a divine tool that we received at Baptism. It's the first of the theological virtues. It has God as the object and the motive. St. Thomas Aquinas, when he tried to analyze the virtue of faith, noticed that there are two moments in the virtue of faith. First, there is what he calls the *inchoatio vitae aeternae*—the beginning of the eternal life. The second moment is when the mind is adapted to accept that which is not evident; it is an encounter of the mind with the mystery.

The first moment—when we exercise faith, the eternal life, the life which is in Heaven—the supernatural life in us is begun anew. When we make an act of faith, there is an ignition of the supernatural life in the soul. The second moment is the overpowering of the mind by God, the First Truth.

Cardinal Avery Dulles suggested that this expression — the beginning of the eternal life — could be translated as the "first installment" of the supernatural life. Every time we make an act of faith, we receive another installment, another encounter, another moment when the power and grace of God pass through Jesus and touch our souls.

Unfortunately, in modern theology the first part of the definition has been effectively shelved and only the second moment was remembered. In modern centuries since the Enlightenment, the question of reason and faith or science and faith has been extensively debated, whereas the first part has been treated as obvious, but it has never really been explained. Why do we need to believe? Why do we need to exercise the faith that we received at Baptism?

Because faith has the capacity to ensure contact with God. When we touch God, God immediately gives Himself. We receive the truths of faith by hearing, and we need the Church's teaching to transmit these truths. In contrast, that first contact that is made with God happens every time we make an act of faith.

On the cover of the book which I wrote for the Year of Faith, there is what is called in French a *bougie*, in Italian a *candella*, and in Polish a *świeca*. The word has two meanings, but not in English. It may mean a candle, but I thought that for the Year of Faith, a book with a candle on the cover would be boring. But the word in Polish, as in Italian and in French, has a dual meaning. It can also mean a spark plug. So, I put a spark plug on the cover! Because every time that we make an act of faith, the supernatural life is triggered; there is the ignition of the supernatural life, and power comes out of Jesus.

There is an inner need of God to give Himself. And acts of faith effectively turn on the switch. When we turn on the switch, the electric power that comes from the power station comes to the lightbulb. When we turn on the switch, we remove an obstacle, and the power comes to the lightbulb. Every time we make an act of faith, we remove the obstacle; we touch the mystery. We believe that Jesus is here, and there is an outpouring of grace. We don't feel it, but Jesus feels it, and like an underground river, there is a movement of grace within us, an inner transformation due to grace. We don't recognize or feel it immediately. But after some time when we have a regular practice of contemplative prayer, we see that the grace of God helps us to untangle difficult problems, to sort out our being, to sort out our moral and emotional problems. There is a fruitfulness of that presence of grace within us, and it passes on to other people whom we encounter.

I like to compare the faith that we receive at Baptism to a computer program. We may have to do something on the computer, but we don't know how to do it. Then we discover, "Hey, I've already got the software on my computer, and I can use it!" And when we use it, there is a moment of joy. There is something extra I can do that I didn't know I could! We receive faith at Baptism, and often we forget about its existence; we don't know what it's for. But when we use faith, there is a moment of joy. When we face various challenges in life, great or small, whether we are looking for a parking spot for our car or some more serious problems, we can exercise faith, opening up to the power of God. But in order to do this, to have this facility of inviting the grace of God into the various moments of our life, we need to practice contemplative prayer regularly, which is the exercise of faith and growth in it.

In her *Autobiographical Manuscripts*, St. Thérèse of Lisieux describes the image of little frail birds which have just been hatched from eggs and are still in the nest. These little birds have big eyes and big hearts. What do they do? They just chirp in their little nest, looking out at the sun. Their only job is to sing to the sun.

But sometimes, dark clouds come, and the sun is hidden. "But in spite of my littleness, I dare to look out toward the divine Son, the Son of Love, and my heart feels the sentiments of an eagle!" St. Thérèse of Lisieux tells us to persevere in our chirping to the sun, in that encounter with God. Even though sometimes there are clouds, there are some distractions, and the mind wanders, when we discover this, we can just return. God doesn't need our beautiful thoughts, our magnificent works. Prayer is not a film with stereophonic music that floats in our imagination.

The simpler this exercise of faith, the better. Often, we have the experience that we come to church, we believe the Blessed Sacrament is here, we kneel or we sit, and we express somehow: "Jesus, I love You." Then the mind wanders. But every time we return and we repeat the act of faith, believing in the supernatural quality of our faith which enables us to touch God, there is an encounter; there is the secret working of God within us.

Thérèse of Lisieux, when still a novice, wrote a letter to her older sister, and she slightly complained that in her prayer, she felt darkness. She says, "Jesus doesn't bother to keep up the conversation. This is a sign that He trusts me." People who know one another don't have to talk all the time. They trust one another. What does this mean? In her moment of prayer, she was experiencing darkness. There is always a contradiction between our natural mind and the supernatural reality of God, so we can persevere in faith only for a certain amount of time. And recognizing that there is a silence, Thérèse says that He doesn't bother to keep up the conversation. Nevertheless, she continues to believe. In the face of darkness, she repeats making deeper acts of faith, renewed acts of faith, touching God.

St. John of the Cross said that we cannot touch God with our senses, with our emotions, with the passions, with the intellect, but only by faith. He describes an image of God as golden but covered with a silver lining. Our reflection and intellectual effort are like the silver lining. If you believe that Jesus is in the Blessed Sacrament and you start thinking how this is possible and you start a philosophical basis of the term used in the theological concept and so on, you are thinking; you are on the level of your reason. You are only touching the concepts of God, the ideas about God, which are like the silver lining.

Whereas, when you set aside this thinking and you make an act of faith—"Jesus, I believe You are here"—you pierce the silver lining and touch the gold which is there. It is extremely important to believe in the supernatural quality of faith. Since faith is supernatural, it is of the same nature as God. It is something divine which is infused in our soul, and we can use it.

Another image described by St. Thérèse is the image of Jesus in the boat with the apostles, and Jesus is asleep. There is a raging storm; they look to Jesus, and He is asleep with His head on a pillow. Thérèse says, "I want to be that pillow." This is an invitation to a deeper faith. An act of faith is conscious. It is not emotional. It is not a question of feelings. It is not intellectual. It is the fruit of received grace. But we can consciously make an act of faith. When we make an act of faith, the fruits are sometimes recognized only a long time afterward. Sometimes when we preach or teach, if we invite God through an act of faith, there is a hidden fruitfulness in what we do.

Recently, I received an e-mail from a friend of mine—we studied together years back. He has five adult daughters. He went to visit one of his daughters who was a postulant in a monastery of Dominican nuns. Now, she is professed. The dad went to see how she was doing. Coming home, he wrote me an e-mail, and he said: "You must have baptized her really hard, because she is very happy there!" I baptized her like a little baby, delicately, gently, as you baptize a little baby. But now she is a Dominican sister, and her father says she was baptized hard. Of course, this is thanks to the fruitfulness of the spiritual life of her family as they brought her up as a good Catholic.

It is important to ensure that we make the time for moments in prayer when we're not talking, when we're not trying to force our emotions, but instead we believe that Jesus is there, and we believe in the supernatural quality of our faith.

Is contemplative prayer difficult? Sometimes we think that there is philosophy, there is metaphysics, and then above that, there is contemplation. No. Children can learn it. Because children are accustomed to the fact that there are things they do not understand, and they accept this in faith. There was a tragic error in catechesis around the 1970s and 1980s (maybe you are an unfortunate victim of that era) when it was suggested that children should not be told things that they cannot understand. For example, they should not be told that there are two natures in Christ, in one Person. Or else, children were required to understand everything we told them. For example: "There are two natures in one Person in Christ, do you understand?" The six-year-old will say, "Yes, I understand" Or, "In God, there are three Persons in one God, do you understand?" They will say yes. But when they are nine years old, they discover that they do not understand, and they reject the truth. It's not a question of forcing them to accept it on reason. But we can take children to church and say, "This is the tabernacle. This is the little home where Jesus lives." But to say that, we have to believe that it is true. If we believe that it's true, and we say this to children, the children will make a moment of prayer—of true contemplative prayer, an exercise of faith, touching God. In fact, it's easier for children to practice faith than for us adults. But we need to do this.

I attended a retreat in France many years back. The priest told us that once he witnessed a group of children being taught by a catechist, a prayerful woman who practiced contemplative prayer. He sat at the back of the church and listened to her telling the children things that children do not understand. She was telling them about the relationships between the Persons within the Trinity. These were seven- or eight-year-olds. The priest at the back could sense that the children were receiving from the lips of the catechist an encounter with the living God. We need to exercise faith.

Aquinas also makes a distinction between an unformed faith and a formed faith. An unformed faith enables us to say that I believe that God exists. *Credo Deum esse.* We can also say that I believe God, that God is truthful. *Credo Deo.* I believe in the truthfulness of the Bible, of the Scriptures, of the teaching of the Church. But this is still an unformed faith.

When faith is formed by charity, we say, *Credo in Deum,* "I believe" toward God. There is a movement. Every time that we make this act of faith toward God, "I believe You are here," there is an outpouring of divine grace. Ultimately, what is important is that we have to live out faith that is operative in love, which is a sign of the working of the Holy Spirit. We need to begin the exercise of faith in silent prayer. Faith grows when it is exercised; it grows by being more and more rooted in the soul. Ultimately, we will develop an almost automatic impulse of inviting God not only into our difficulties, but also into our work and rest.

Several years back when I preached a retreat for nuns in Nashville, I gave an example. I then met one of the Sisters of Life, who asked me, "Father, when you preached to the sisters in Nashville [because what I said was recorded, and these things wander between communities], what did you mean when you said that?" I had given the example of airports, but in the meantime, airports have changed. In the restrooms in airports, there were taps, but not the ones that you turn as I turned them on in my childhood, where you turned the tap, and the water was running. Then there were taps that you had to press, and as you pressed, the water ran, and when you stopped pressing it, it stopped running. Now, it is all electronic. You just wave your fingers, and the water flows. But basically, what I wanted to say by this example of the tap is that you have to press, and the water flows. Like pressing a water tap, when you make an act of faith and persevere in it, the grace of God starts to flow; there is an effusion of God's grace.

I do not know to what extent this is the case in America, but in Poland there is a very deep-rooted and unconscious heresy of semi-Pelagianism. Pelagianism is a heresy which claims that we don't need grace, whereas semi-Pelagianism is a heresy which says that we need grace, but the first moment is natural, is human, and that by our own effort we can transfer ourselves to the supernatural life. This is a heresy. Faith is a gift of God. It is not from us. We receive faith at Baptism and sometimes even before Baptism. Faith is not the fruit of good arguments, experiences, or a World Youth Day. No, faith is a gift of God.

Faith also is not the fruit of a good example. Priests are told they must give a good example, and then lay people will believe. What do the laity know about the life of priests? It is not a question of a priest making a show of himself.

Faith is a divine gift, but it is a very fragile gift. It is hidden but also extremely resistant. A pond can teem with fish and bugs and life in it, but after a hot summer, the pond dries up. You can walk on the floor of the pond; there is nothing there; it is like a desert. Then suddenly, the rain comes, and the pond again teems with life. The life was hidden, and it comes back. The faith that we have received is extremely fragile; it is hidden, but it is resistant.

Sometimes you have people who, seemingly for years on end, have no faith; they even declare themselves to be atheists. They have not exercised faith, but they had received it at Baptism, and in a dramatic moment, suddenly it wakes up in them. In particular, this happens when they are surrounded by people who believe, and these people invite the Holy Spirit Who is inhabiting the soul of the person with whom they are speaking, even though this may be a difficult teenager or a person who claims not to believe in anything. But if you invite the Holy Spirit, Who lives in the heart of those to whom you are speaking, and you speak to them in faith, suddenly this hidden, dried-up life wakes up, and there is a movement. You may not immediately see the reactions, but there is an effusion of grace there.

Prayer is the exercise of faith. It is not a question of feelings. But if you search, looking for God, pleading, yearning, you do this because you have already been moved by God.

First of all, we have to practice the theological virtues—faith, hope, and charity—and faith is the first among them. Moral perfection is not necessary for the exercise of faith and the love of God. Today, there is an erroneous trend in thinking that first you must enter a stage of asceticism to purify the soul by your own effort. The mystical stage then comes in old age when you are well-organized and well-behaved. No, there may be disorder in a person on the level of the emotions. There may be disorder in the moral life, and yet you can make true acts of faith, touching God. There may be true weaknesses and blunders in your life, but as you make acts of faith, "I believe" toward God, you touch Jesus like that woman with her finger, and the grace of Jesus comes.

Do not leave the mystical stage to old age, but begin now on the basis of the graces you have received at Baptism. God sometimes leaves within us some difficulty, some thorn of the flesh that St.

Paul had, to keep us humble, to remind us that we need the grace of God. The grace of God may not automatically heal everything. There may be some weaknesses left. We experience our poverty; it may be our emotional poverty, our moral poverty, or our spiritual poverty. When you meet your family or friends, you may have no words; you don't know how to convince them, how to reach them, and you perceive your limitations. All these moments of our poverty are useful if we treat them like a trampoline and we bounce off them into the arms of God. We make acts of faith in the context of our weakness.

Faith, of course, needs to be nourished, and the Gospels tell us about three nourishments of faith: The first nourishment is the Eucharist: "Anyone who eats this bread will live forever" (John 6:51). The second nourishment is the Word of God: "Man does not live on bread alone but on every word that comes from the mouth of God" (Matthew 4:4). And then the third nourishment is doing the will of God. Jesus said, "My food is to do the will of the One who sent Me" (John 4:34).

In our modern world, there is a profound distortion caused by Gnosticism. True faith requires humility of the intellect. As I said, there are two moments: the triggering of the life of grace within us, and the adapting of the mind toward the life-giving mystery, which has been revealed and given to us. We need to accept the truths revealed in Scriptures and in Church teachings; some are mysterious and should remain as such. We cannot fully understand the truths of faith. We can think within faith, and we can arrive at catechetical formulae, but always the mystery has to remain. Gnosticism, in contrast, is prideful. It places the intellect above faith and looks down on the faith of simple people.

This is the deepest source of the crisis we are seeing in the Church in country after country, particularly since Vatican II. We have seen attempts to scan the divinely revealed mystery through criteria that come from outside the mystery, such as philosophy, archeology, linguistics, comparative religions, psychology, sociology, political projects of the Left or of the Right, and ideas concerning pastoral relevance along the lines of: "There are truths of faith, but we'll drop most of them; we'll pick out only those that we think are relevant according to our criteria, if they fit our opinions about archeology, linguistics, or our political projects. If it doesn't, we drop it."

This is the supermarket approach. When you enter the supermarket, you do not buy everything on the shelves. You pick a few things you need, and you ignore the rest. Whereas in faith, we cannot do that. If that is what we do, it means our intellect and our own criteria are superior than the mystery which has been revealed and has been transmitted by the Church since the times of the apostles. This represents a profound intellectual pride, a mindset that says, "We know better which fragments of Scriptures to accept and which to reject, which dogmatic statements please us and which we drop." No, we are not to scan the truths of faith according to criteria coming from this world, but we have to do the reverse. We have to scan our lives through the ultimate criteria, which is the divinely revealed mystery. We have to base ourselves on the mystery.

The more we grow in our faith, the more the mystery becomes mysterious, becomes dark until we learn, like St. Peter, how to walk on water. When Peter believed that Jesus was the Son of God, he walked; when he stopped believing, he began to sink. We have to have the courage to base ourselves on the solid foundation, which is walking on water. There is the mystery of faith that we accept, and as we do so, we grow in faith. It is not true that difficulties and darkness are a result of our sins—"First polish your souls, get rid of your sins, and when you are ideal, then everything will be clear." No, the darkness is a result of the incompatibility between our intellect, which is natural, and the mystery, which is greater than the capacity of our intellect. It is as if there is a contradiction between the natural and the supernatural.

We can conquer the mystery only by making further acts of faith, enabled by received grace. This is how we encounter God. So always there is a certain darkness, and there is no point in dreaming that at some moment everything will all become clear and simple. As we advance in life, it is in the challenges, the sicknesses, the difficulties, the cancer, the family problems, and so on that we encounter the mystery. We are not to panic but rather make acts of faith, which penetrate the mystery, believing that these acts of faith touch God.

Of course, there is a place for thinking. We do not deny the dignity of the reason. Faith is the humility of the intellect and not the amputation of the intellect. The intellect is valuable; it is good. We can think outside faith, in the realms of philosophy and the sciences, and we can also think within faith, the *cogitatio fidei*, the thinking within faith, searching for the intelligibility of faith, the inner coherence, but not the proof. We cannot have proof. We believe in the Resurrection, because we believe God, not because we have become convinced because of studies made on the Shroud of Turin, because of what physicists have said about its composition. That is not why we believe in the Resurrection. There is nothing wrong with such studies made on the Shroud of Turin. But even if it were fake, it is irrelevant. Our faith is based on the mystery.

We can think within faith, and we can arrive at a theology, a coherent presentation of the mysteries, looking for their intelligibility and not their rationality. We're not trying to prove that it is all rational, understandable, comprehendible, or that we have proof as such. Instead, we look for the intelligibility, the inner coherence, we try to see how the truths all fit together, how they correspond to the hunger of our intellect. But yet they remain mysterious.

St. Gregory the Great said about St. Thomas the Apostle after the Resurrection that he saw a man with wounds, and rationally, he probably said, "We have to call an ambulance with such wounds and do something about them." But in his faith, he said, "My Lord and my God." And so, he says, "*Aliud vidit, et aliud credidit*" – "He saw one thing; he believed in another." He saw a man with wounds; he believed: "My Lord and my God."

It's important not to mix the discourses coming from the sciences and from faith. The Council of Chalcedon said that in Christ there are two natures, the human and the divine, which are distinct and unmixed. Faith and the sciences also have to be distinct and unmixed. There must be a primacy of the mystery of faith in our lives. So, we do not prove that the theory of evolution is wrong on the basis of arguments taken from the Scriptures. We have to demand arguments and proofs on the level of science. This is not a question of faith; it is a question of science, and if there is something missing, then study it, look for it, but do not mix the two. We do not prove the truths of faith, we do not prove the presence of Jesus in the Holy Sacrament on the basis of biological or DNA analysis or a chemical analysis of the Host. No, we keep the two distinct. Distinct and unmixed.

We need to maintain the primacy of the mystery and the exercise of faith in our lives. That is why it is important to have a rhythm of contemplative prayer. Not intellectual contemplation, which may be philosophical, ascetical, or mathematic, whereby we look and wonder at the truth, or if we see a beautiful view, we think, "Wow, it's wonderful," or how a mathematician may be touched by the beauty of a complex formula. This is purely intellectual. Rather, in faith there is a simple intuition of the divine Person.

We need to struggle more to enter into a relationship with God than to free ourselves from sin. That's why we need moments of private prayer and adoration of the Blessed Sacrament. Everyone has a different rhythm, but in the rhythm of our own life, we have to find a moment to pray. Sometimes, people like the morning. Others prefer praying in the evening or at midday, by dropping into a church or at home praying in front of a little icon or something. We have to find our own method, our own rhythm. It's not a question of feeding the imagination, looking for psychic ease, being at ease with oneself, nor is it a question of intellectual effort, of trying to understand the truths logically. Rather, it's about facing the mystery and believing that the mystery is penetrated by our faith even though Jesus seems to be asleep or He doesn't try to keep up the conversation. We need to habituate ourselves to persevere in the face of this darkness, repeating acts of faith, believing in their power to touch God. This means generating a space for God in our soul.

The time for prayer has to be organized, or else it is the first thing you give up when you have little time. Often a priest, when he has no time, the first thing he gives up is prayer. Then he gives up his friends. In our daily life, we need to maintain a lively contact with God. This precedes any activity, any apostolate. If you do not pray, then whatever mission you have becomes useless; it becomes insipid. You are a natural do-gooder with pride.

Often, we need to exercise faith during the liturgy. People recognize when a priest is prayerful (in Poland, they say, "This is a believing priest," suggesting that other priests are not particularly believing). People recognize if the priest is prayerful, if he prays in private. If he prays in private, then the liturgy is celebrated in a prayerful way. If you attend a liturgy celebrated by a priest who obviously does not pray much, and he celebrates in a mechanical way, add your faith, sitting in the pews where you are. Believe in the truthfulness in what he is celebrating. Or if the readers and the choir are all concentrated on themselves, trying to change the liturgy into a concert, you believe. Exercise your faith.

Cardinal Sarah was very shocked when he attended the World Meeting of Families in Philadelphia in September 2015. He saw priests, who were concelebrating the Mass, taking pictures of themselves as they came up to receive Communion. This is tragic. These things happen. If you see something like this, make an act of faith. Pray for them, believing that your faith touches God.

CONFERENCE 2

Being a Child Before God

"Blessed be the God and Father of our Lord Jesus Christ, who has blessed us in Christ with every spiritual blessing in the heavens, as He chose us in Him before the foundation of the world to be holy and without blemish before Him.

In love, He destined us for adoption to Himself

through Jesus Christ in accord with the favor

of His will for the praise of the glory of His

grace that He granted us in the Beloved."

— Ephesians 1:3–6

This long text of the hymn of St. Paul has no punctuation in the Greek text that we have in the New Testament. There are no commas, no full stops. There are several themes in these lines, but apparently the point of the message is that we become the adopted children of God through our Brother, Jesus Christ. The important message is that God chose us before the creation of the world. Before the sin of Adam, before our own sin, God chose us. The elective love of God precedes Creation, precedes our existence and our sins. God's paternal love contains a project for each one of us. God does not give up His plans because of our personal history. Human nature is encompassed within the divine project. This perspective is clear in the writings of St. Paul and in the great theologians, like St. Irenaeus and St. Thomas Aquinas.

But somehow in modern theology, this was shelved, and the point of departure or reflection was either creation and nature and the natural law, or sometimes in the Augustinian tradition, everything seems to begin with the sin of Adam and the repairing of the consequences of that sin. Whereas clearly St. Paul says that God chose us before the foundation of the world. This means our human nature is encompassed in the loving concern of God the Father. We have to view nature *within* this divine project.

In modern centuries, nature and grace have come to be conceived of as two decks of a London bus, as if nature were the lower deck with something added onto it. But a bus can function very well with just one deck, so nature was seen to be self-explanatory and self-sufficient. We can reflect upon nature philosophically, and we can see its coherence. In contrast, grace is wonderful; but it was seen as an *extra* gift which is seen as optional, something added on. In this understanding, moral reflection is typically based on philosophy, on the natural law, on the external life with its individual acts. Whereas the life of grace, the encounter with God, is viewed as wonderful but belonging to a separate discipline: spiritual theology, sometimes called the theology of the interior life. It is seen as something optional, good for chosen souls and contemplative nuns. The upper deck of a London bus gives you a better view, but you can also travel on the lower deck.

Vatican II didn't follow this model. It returned to the vision of St. Paul, St. Irenaeus, and the great masters. There is only one divine project, and nature is within the divine project. Nature has its consistencies and its coherence, which we can perceive. It can be viewed rationally, explained, understood, and so we respect philosophy. But our God-given vocation is deeper. It precedes the creation of nature. We are called to a mysterious encounter with the heavenly Father through our Brother, Jesus Christ. The Spirit working in our souls leads us to Christ. We relate to Him in faith and love, and through Him we discover His Father and our Father. Jesus is the way to the heavenly Father.

The gift of faith is a tool received at Baptism, which enables us to engage in a relationship with the Persons of the Trinity. This gift of faith had also been given *before* the Incarnation, in the Old

Testament, when the relationship with God was much more difficult. The temple in Jerusalem focused on divine transcendence, and there was always a temptation to search for idols that have a more imaginable face.

Even outside the history of salvation—within natural religiosity among the people of the American continent, before Columbus, and long before even Christ, before Abraham—God sometimes gave the grace of faith, which enabled people to believe in God and respond to Him. But that gift, if it was given, was deeply immersed within a completely natural religiosity. So, we do not exclude the possibility that outside the history of salvation, some people have reacted to God, to His grace with their love, with their response.

But with Christ, we can focus our faith; we can imagine Him. God has appeared with a human face. Through Christ, we are introduced into the divine mystery, and we can recognize the Father. When this perspective of our relationship with the Father and our divine adoption was forgotten, sometime in the fourteenth century, Christian art started to depict images of the Father with things like a long beard ... terrifying. This is always wrong! Whenever we try to depict the Father, we always get it wrong—a terrifying old man.

Before the fourteenth century, the Father was never painted in Christian art, because Christ is the image of the invisible Father. In the cathedrals, you had Christ on the front door, and in the mosaics, you had Christ the Pantocrator, whereas the Father was hidden. We learn the Father through Christ. The Father is somehow mysterious, and we can say that God hides in the mystery. But by hiding in the mystery, He reveals Himself more, because we encounter God, not through our clear, rational knowledge, but through faith and love, where there is trust and a recognition of the paternal heart. God was mysterious, and St. Paul was very much aware that the mysterious, divine plan has been disclosed.

If you have a moment, read Ephesians 1–3, where Paul shows that he was aware of the fact that he was a servant of a divine mystery that now had been revealed. He writes that is why we are bold enough to approach God in complete confidence through our faith in Christ. We can trust in the paternity of God because we have seen it at work in the heart of Jesus.

In the center of the Christian message is our filiation, our becoming the sons and daughters of the heavenly Father through our Brother as adopted children. We are called to be the children of God, and this is not a reward for good living that is granted at some final stage. It's a divine gift that precedes our existence; it is the project of God that precedes the creation of the world. This call to be the children of God—to live out our lives as the children of the heavenly Father—continues in spite of our complicated lives and the errors that we have committed. The central issue is, what does all this mean?

St. Paul teaches us this in Romans 8:14, "Those are the children of God who are moved by the Spirit of God," just as Jesus was moved by the Spirit of God when He was sent to the world and when He was sent to the desert. We read that He was moved by the Spirit of God. We are called to be moved by the same Spirit. Those are the children of God, who are attentive to the movement of the Holy Spirit. *Hi sunt filii Dei, qui Spiritu Dei aguntur* (there are various Latin versions, but I prefer this one).

We live out the divine sonship when we perceive the movements of the Holy Spirit and react to them; when we recognize that we are being led by the Spirit and we willingly accept this. So, this is the main concern of the Church: Do we recognize the suggestions of the Holy Spirit? Do we want to listen to them? Do we react to them? Do we allow ourselves to be led? Or do we impose upon God our own projects? What is the impact of this revealed, mysterious truth in our lives?

Again, in Ephesians 3:14-19, Paul said, "I pray kneeling before the Father, from whom every family where the spiritual or natural takes its name. Out of His infinite glory, may He give you the power through His Spirit for your hidden self to grow strong so that Christ may live in your hearts through faith and then planted in love and built on love. You, with all the saints, have strength to grasp the breadth and the length, the height and the depth until knowing the love of Christ, which is beyond all knowledge, you are filled by the utter fullness of God."

We are drawn into the family of the blessed Trinity, and our inner self, our interior life, what makes us tick from within, is strengthened by the power of the Holy Spirit. We attach ourselves to Christ by faith and love—exercising faith, animated by love—in prayer. Then immediately, the power—the gift of the Holy Spirit comes through Jesus and fills our heart. As a result, we acquire a breadth of vision, which goes beyond the tight, limited perspective of human ideologies. We have a wide perspective, because we view everything from the perspective of the heart of the Father.

We have a long perspective. We view things with longanimity. Longanimity is the virtue of teachers. Teachers teach kids, and they never get any gratitude from them. When the time for gratitude comes, it is forty years later, when the teachers are frail and in an elderly home. It is at that moment when the kids they taught realize that they have learned something wonderful from their teachers. The teacher does not expect immediate results, knowing they will come in time. When we view things with length, we have a long-distance approach. We do not panic as a result of immediate difficulties, because we have this capacity for patience and perseverance and long-waiting.

We view things from the height. We perceive ourselves and others from the height of the cross of Jesus, from the perspective of His Divine Redemptive Mercy which is given to us freely.

We have depth; we are not superficial, because we base ourselves on the power of God working within us and working in others. Thus, we are filled with the utter fullness of God. This is the perspective with which Paul was praying for us.

We can think of three possible approaches to God. The philosopher reflects upon reality, upon life, upon being, on the cosmos, metaphysics. The philosopher arrives at the conclusion that some absolute, subsistent being must exist, a being that has existence from nobody else but from himself. So, the point of departure of the philosopher is his own reflecting reason. He tries to understand reality, and if he is honest in his search, he may arrive at the conclusion: there must be some absolute prime mover, some ultimate end. But this does not say much about God. Certainly, the philosopher, with some difficulty, may arrive at the conclusion that God exists, but this is still not everything.

The theologian has the Bible, has divine revelation, the Scriptures. The theologian receives the Scriptures in faith and tries to fathom the meaning of the Word of God; he tries to fathom the history of salvation, how God worked through the history of the chosen people and in the Church. For the theologian, the point of departure is the gift of faith, which has conditioned his mind and adapted him to accept the revealed truth and the contents of that faith given in revelation and transmitted by the Church. The theologian receives this and thinks within his faith. He tries to understand. He thinks and ponders within the faith and arrives at clear conclusions, at the articles of faith and at the truths in the *Catechism*, which structure the mind and help us develop convictions and clarity in our decision-making.

There also is a third possibility: the contemplative person, who tastes the reality of God in direct experience. Both the philosopher and the theologian stand outside of God, on the threshold of God, but they do not yet taste the divine life from within. Whereas we, as the adopted children of God, are called to something more, to encounter God from within.

We can compare these three approaches to somebody who wants to know something about a certain family. The philosopher is like somebody who has a picture, a photograph, of a family. He can study the photograph, seeing that there's a father, a mother, children, and the pet dog. He can know something about a family by a photo of that family. He can know some truth about that family by looking at it. He can guess the age of the children and so on. So, there are some truths we can know by looking at a photo, but we know very little.

Whereas the theologian's approach is like that of a historian studying the archives of a family; he may learn a great deal from the family archives. Sometimes noble, aristocratic families have great archives, and a historian may study all the details. He may find out things that even the present members of the family do not know. But he is still outside the family.

Whereas the contemplative is like a child that is adopted into a family. The adopted child may not know the archives or the history of the family into which it is received. But the child knows the family from within, as the adopted child, through the perspective of love. This is what God is proposing to us. This is what God wants for us, that we be the adopted children of God.

In the Blessed Trinity there is life. There is the flame of divine love. God is love, and there is the eternal generation of the divine

Word, the Son, and the flame of love deriving from them, the Holy Spirit. The flame of fire is as if it were searching for nourishment. Fire has the capacity that it wants to burn, like the forest fires in California. It expands like the divine love looking for souls it can consume.

Since God is alive, we do not base ourselves uniquely on the metaphysical principle, *agere sequitur esse* (action follows being), but also on the *agere sequitur vita* (our action follows the life), the life of the Trinity. God's action flows from the inner life of God, and in God there is joy. And that joy is eternal.

Jesus told us that there is more joy in giving than in receiving. When He told us this, it was not just a moral command. Jesus spoke from the inner experience of the Trinity. This is something we can also experience, and even small children can experience the joy of giving. I am sure you have often had in your life moments in which you have given something freely and you have found a joy in the fact that you have given freely. The Holy Trinity has the inner desire to give, to give freely. Whenever Jesus found souls which were humble and open to receive the divine gift, He spoke about the joy of the Trinity: "Blessed are You, Father in the Spirit." He spoke expressing the joy of the Trinity. This divine joy is the cause and end of everything.

The Creation of the world was also a moment of joy for God. We can imagine Adam viewing the entire procession of animals coming up to him and giving each one a name. He saw a little animal and said, "You will be called a panda." And then to another little being, "You shall be called a chipmunk." God experienced joy in the Creation. Even more, God wants *us* to share in His eternal love, in the joy of the love of God, Who wants to give. We are called to participate in that joy because we are the children of God.

Somehow in the modern centuries, this was forgotten. Moral theology was centered on law, on obligations, on duties, on commandments, on sins we have to avoid. In France, there was the current of Jansenism in the eighteenth century, which emphasized respect and projected human ideas about justice onto God but with no spirituality, and this generated fear.

As a reaction to this, we have the deism of the eighteenth-century philosophers. They observed order in the world, which they attributed to some god, some creator, some clockmaker, who established the world, but who created the world and then went to sleep, being unconcerned about the world. This was a purely rational perception of order.

In these approaches, there was no mysticism, no encounter with the living God, no participation in the joy of God. Such a religiosity was dry, and this led to the French Revolution, which was a reaction against such a religiosity. We need to perceive the inner life of God and learn how to be a child before God. In recent times, we have had two powerful voices rebelling against such a dry spirituality: the voices of St. Thérèse of Lisieux and St. Faustina Kowalska.

St. Thérèse heard invitations to offer herself to divine justice as reparation for the sins of the world. This was the spirituality that she was hearing in her convent. "We have to do penance because the world is horrible, full of sin, but we are the good souls. The justice of God is so terrible that it requires our penance because the world is so horrible." There is a pride in this way of thinking. St. Thérèse rebelled against such preaching, as well as the attitude of her superior in her convent.

She said, "No, it's not a question of reparation for sin in the name of justice, but openness to Divine Mercy." This is the central core of her message. She recognized that God is love. She recognized this through her own spiritual experience. She rejected this distortion of God which made a terrible judge out of God. She offered herself to divine love, to be an instrument of divine love, not out of obedience, not out of respect for God, but for the good pleasure of God. God has a joy, has fun when He gives His grace, when He finds souls that are willing to accept His love. God can expand the inner life of the Trinity; this is a moment of joy for God, allowing God to have that moment of fun, that moment of joy, of being happy as a result of His gift. She wanted to be an instrument of that love. She saw that God finds joy in the work that He does in a human soul. She wanted to participate in that joy of God as the divine love takes over human souls.

She was less concerned about divine glory and more concerned about giving to God moments of joy, the joy that God can experience when He meets with no internal opposition, no excluding obstacle erected by the human soul. She seemed to perceive the trepidation of the divine heart, the heart of Jesus in the face of the Samaritan woman, the woman caught in adultery, the father of the Prodigal Son. She saw these moments of inner joy of the divine heart, when mercy is given, when it is diffused. She wanted to offer to God an occasion for divine love to give.

The message of St. Faustina Kowalska is similar, focusing on Divine Mercy. But I think she was more influenced by preachers who stressed justice and a sense of reparation. Also, Sister Faustina had visions, whereas I have no visions. She had a vision of Jesus and was called to paint a painting, whereas I do not have visions, and I presume you don't have visions either. So, I find the road of St. Thérèse closer to our experience. Because we do not have visions, we encounter God in faith and love, and this is what she teaches.

God finds joy that goes beyond merit and justice. St. Thérèse writes, "I know that the Lord is infinitely just, and it is this justice which terrifies so many people. But this justice is the object of my joy and confidence. Because to be just means not only to be severe in the punishment of the culpable but also to recognize good intentions and reward virtue. I expect as much from the justice of the good God as from His mercy."

She makes another comparison, that of an infant peacefully sleeping at the heart of a general (you can imagine a general in the army who has a baby asleep at his heart). By that heart, we can learn courage, and above all, trust. What is artillery fire, the explosion of guns, when you are being carried by a general? These are wonderful images showing the beauty of mercy and divine trust.

To be small means never to be discouraged.

HOMILY 2

The Dance of the Adolescent

"Herod, the tetrarch, heard of the reputation of Jesus and said to his servants, 'This man is John the Baptist. He has been raised from the dead. That is why mighty powers are at work in him.' Now Herod had arrested John, bound him and put him in prison on account of Herodias, the wife of his brother, Philip. For John had said to him, 'It is not lawful for you to have her.' Although he wanted to kill him, he feared the people, for they regarded him as a prophet. But at a birthday celebration for Herod, the daughter of Herodias performed a dance before the guests and delighted Herod so much that he swore to give her whatever she might ask for.

Prompted by her mother, she said, 'Give me here on a platter the head of John the Baptist.' The king was distressed, but because of his oath, and the guests who were present, he ordered that it be given, and he had John beheaded in the prison. The head was brought in on a platter and given to the girl, who took it to her mother. His disciples took away the corpse and buried him, and they went and told Jesus."

— Matthew 14:1–12

Not only Herod found the dancing girl charming. I, too, think that she was charming, that she was graceful. At this Eastern birthday banquet with all the guests, the teenage girl came out and danced. She put everything into the dance, and the dance was touching. The people present noticed that there was something special in this dance. Since they had drank a lot of alcohol, they could not really understand what it was. But remember, this teenage girl was the daughter of a broken marriage. Her mother had dropped her husband, and now she had a new partner—King Herod.

This teenage girl, age twelve or thirteen, danced before the new partner of her mother. And in that dance, she put in all the pain of her broken heart. She pleaded as she danced. She was pleading that Herod would be a father for her because she was at the age when a teenage girl needs a dad who is attentive, who listens to her chatter, who answers her adolescent questions, who gives some direction in life. She felt alone because she had no father. Her mother had dropped the father. And so, she pleaded with the new partner: Be a substitute dad for me. This pain and suffering of her heart expressed itself in her muscles as she danced.

Those present did not understand the issue. Only her mother, Herodias, did. She immediately understood what was happening. With her motherly heart, she saw what was happening in the heart of her daughter. The Letter to the Hebrews says that the Word of God is alive like a two-edged sword penetrating the point where the soul meets the body. The Word of God penetrates the human interior. God has spoken in various ways in the history of salvation. This time, God spoke through the muscles of that dancing girl. And the mother immediately understood.

The conscience is the act of reason, and the conscience of Herodias worked well. She immediately understood. Herodias is the only negative character among the women in the New Testament. All the other women are positive characters, including the wife of Pilate. Herodias immediately understood the issue, because her conscience reacted well. But after the judgment of conscience comes free choice, the decision of what to do. Herodias was faced with a challenge. She immediately understood what her daughter needed, and she could have decided to take her daughter and return to her husband. But she decided instead to ask for the head of the prophet, who had the courage to speak out in the defense of the indissolubility of a natural, pagan, nonsacramental marriage.

Hope

"One of them, named Cleopas, said to him in reply, 'Are you the only visitor to Jerusalem who does not know of the things that have taken place there in these days?' And he replied to them, 'What sort of things?' They said to him, 'The things that happened to Jesus the Nazarene, who was a prophet, mighty in deed and word, before God and all the people. How our chief priests and rulers both handed Him over to a sentence of death and crucified Him. But we were hoping that He would be the one to redeem Israel. And besides all this, it is now the third day since this took place. Some women from our group, however, have astounded us.

They were at the tomb early in the morning and did

not find His body. They came back and reported

that they had indeed seen a vision of angels, who

announced that He was alive. Then some of those

with us went to the tomb and found things just as

the women had described, but Him they did not see.'

And he said to them, 'Oh, how foolish you are; how

slow of heart to believe all that the prophets spoke.

Was it not necessary that the Messiah should suffer

these things and enter into His glory?' Then beginning

with Moses and all the prophets, He interpreted to

them what referred to Him in all the scriptures."

— Luke 24:18–27

The disciples were walking to Emmaus. They had hope in Jesus, and that hope was shattered. It turned out that they had hoped in their own way, not in the way of God. Their hopes were political. They were expecting a political messiah who would resolve social and political problems, and they read the Scriptures in this vein. Even though they recognized the extraordinary power and role of Jesus, they didn't understand anything. They were blind. And that is why they were depressed when things did not turn out as they had expected.

Jesus called them foolish. Whoever is locked in his own ideas is foolish. In His response, Jesus made a reference to the eternal divine project of the heavenly Father, confirming what St. Paul wrote, "God chose us before the creation of the world and predestined us to be God's adopted children" (Ephesians 1:4). St. Peter in his letter tells us that we have been redeemed, "The ransom has been paid, and the precious blood of a lamb without spot or stain, namely Christ, who though known since before the world was made, has been revealed only in our time, the end of ages, for your sake" (1 Peter 1:18-20).

We need to view everything, including our own projects and hopes, in the light of the eternal divine project. God did not plan a scenario in which sin was scheduled. The divine plan is one in which we participate in the divine life as adopted children of the Trinity. But as a result of sin, the drama became a tragedy but with a happy end. We have been saved by the spotless, impeccable Lamb.

We can explain the mystery of the Redemption by imagining a religious sister who, as a missionary, is sent to a distant country where she is killed. She dies as a martyr, and her parents are informed about their daughter's death. Emotionally, of course, they are sad. But if they are spiritual people, on a deeper level they may experience a certain spiritual joy. That love that they taught their daughter had won in her heart. They remember when she was a little girl, when they taught her to be generous toward her brother and not to eat all the chocolate, and they observed the growth of virtues in her. Now they see that she has given herself totally. Love has won in her heart. She has remained faithful to that supreme love to the very end.

This is how the heavenly Father views Jesus' total gift of Self. Seeing the power of divine love in the heart of Jesus, the Father is well-pleased. He says, "This is My beloved Son, in whom is the totality of My love" (Matthew 3:17). The total gift of Self of Jesus — the spotless Lamb who, though killed, lives forever — is our salvation. The direct cause of His death on the Cross was His torturers. But the indirect cause was His gift of Self. Aquinas asked the question, "Did Jesus commit suicide?" We can raise this question. He answers by making a distinction between the direct and indirect cause. He asks, "If we leave a book on the windowsill and it gets soaked in the rain, what is the direct cause?" The direct cause is the rain, which soaked the book. But the indirect cause is you who left the book on the windowsill, allowing it to get soaked. Aquinas says, "The direct cause were the torturers who crucified Jesus. But the indirect cause was His gift of Self. Jesus gave Himself freely, thereby manifesting the magnitude of divine love."

The Father gives us His Son Who, with this maximum sign of charity, gave Himself to us. We can hook onto Him in our faith. We have a natural sense of justice, and we do not want a cheap grace. We know that evil should be somehow repaired. Our natural sense of justice is fulfilled by Jesus' total gift of Self. The Father is well-pleased that He has given His Son, "There's more joy in giving than in receiving" (Acts 20:35). The Father has given us the Son and told us that we can be freed of our sins if we hook onto Him. We are drawn into that same divine love which brings us into the life of the Trinity. Those are the children of God who are led by the Holy Spirit, the love of the Trinity.

To grow into the life and love of God as children, we need to purify our hope. We have an inkling of this in the parable of the merciful father of the Prodigal Son. The Prodigal Son was an interesting character. He had a left-wing perspective. He did not believe in original sin. He was interested in the world. He imposed upon the father his own idea. He said to the father, "Give me what I have a right to inherit." We know the rest of the story. With his left-wing attitude, he went abroad to a distant country and spent all his money. His human hopes and projects turned out to be a failure. But at least we can say he was an interesting individual. He wanted something in life. He was curious about the world.

Whereas the older brother had a right-wing approach. He did not believe in the mercy of the father. He held onto the rules, the law, the sense of justice. He also imposed his ideas upon the father. He did his work. He was paid his wage. He ate his food rations. He went to work again. He was paid again. That was his sense of justice. He could not imagine the mercy of the father.

Both brothers were locked in their own ideas, and they failed to perceive their father's love. Now, I don't know if you noticed, but there is a third, hidden brother in the parable. He is the one who did not impose anything upon the father. He did not treat his equality with the father as a right, but he emptied himself and assumed the condition of a slave. Here, I am quoting Philippians 2. Jesus Christ is the hidden third brother in the parable. It's about Him, the servant in the parable, who the prodigal dreamed about when he was feeding the pigs. He was the extension of the father's heart and hand. He received the prodigal brother when he came and washed his feet. He prepared the banquet for the celebration of the father's mercy. He fell into conflict with the older brother, the right-wing one. He is the one who said, "The father and I are one."

The third brother, mysteriously hidden in the parable, models the way for the Church. Is not this the way Pope Francis is trying to show us, the way of the third brother who is the extension of the eyes and the heart of the father? He's the one who prepared the liturgy for the celebration of the return of the Prodigal Son. The two brothers were locked in their respective ideologies, the right-wing and the left-wing. These ideologies prevented them from recognizing the father's heart. Ideologies are human hopes that we try to impose upon God; we try to force God to do things according to our way. As we persist in them, we are foolish because we fall out of a filial relationship with the Father. That is why Jesus called the disciples on the way to Emmaus "foolish."

We need to allow ourselves to be led by God into His mystery, to be led by His way. This entails a purification of hope. What is hope?

Aquinas makes a distinction, noting four different types of hope. First of all, hope is an emotion. Animals have emotions, and we have emotions. Hope is a healthy ambition; it is the emotional force to get something done. Some people have a strong emotional hope. Other people are a bit weak in this; that is how our temperament is made. Let's take the antelopes, which run across the savannah in Africa. Suddenly, there's a stream. One jumps across the stream, the other stops because the stream is too big. The one which has the hope, the healthy ambition, jumps; whereas the other one who stops is afraid. Some people have this internal zip to face challenges, to get things done. Others are slow. This derives from our temperament. We cannot change our temperament, but we can form our character. The temperament is given; it is the psychic structure of every individual. This is the first type of hope, which is not a virtue. It is just a psychic force of our emotion.

Second, there is hope as a moral virtue. In the Polish language, the word for "hope" (*nadzieja*) basically means "toward action"—the force to act. Etymologically, the word means "a force to get something done." In the presentation of Aristotle and Aquinas, the moral virtue of hope is located not only in the emotion of hope but also partly in the will; it is traditionally called magnanimity. It is the summoning of our psychic forces in view of some action. The object of this moral virtue is some good that we want to attain: a good job, a pleasant holiday, an election victory for our political candidate. The opposite of this virtue is the vice of pusillanimity, which is like the dropping of the hands and saying, "Well, what's the point of doing something; it won't work anyway." If you lack the moral virtue of hope and you stop doing anything because there is no point, then nothing gets done. We need the moral virtue of hope to get things done. This hope as a natural virtue is an acquired virtue that the ancient philosophers knew and described.

If we live in the life of grace, this moral virtue of hope that we can cultivate within us is transformed. Within the life of grace—where there is an encounter with God in the theological virtues of faith, hope, and charity—this acquired moral virtue is transformed. It becomes the infused virtue of magnanimity. It still has some temporal object: a good job, a pleasant holiday, an election victory for our political candidate. But if this is the will of God, Aquinas says this is *tamen sub Deo* (but under God). I have this dynamism propelling me to do things, but I accept divine providence, which is greater than my own force. This virtue gives the strength to act but within faith and trust in God.

There is a fourth type of hope—the hope that is the theological virtue infused by grace. It has God, the living, mysterious God, recognized in faith, as its object. This infused virtue of hope is located in the human will, adapting that will to the mysterious plans of God, which are unfolding in our lives. We need to accept that God is leading us and revealing His divine mystery step by step. Through the virtue of hope, we accept this, wanting what God wants for us. The disciples on the way to Emmaus had to have their hope purified so as to accept a mystery that was much greater than their expectations. They were expecting a political success, and their hope had to be purified to something greater.

As we live out the virtue of hope, we touch God, as is the case with the exercise of faith. The woman suffering from the hemorrhage, who touched Jesus' cloak with her finger, touched Jesus by her faith and also by her hope. She touched Jesus, and power came out of Jesus. Hope also touches God. When the theological virtues are lived out, they overlap. Theoretically, we can distinguish and name them. But in practical life, they intermingle. Hope, as a theological virtue, springs from faith and leads to charity. Hope involves the acceptance of the divine mystery as it unfolds in our lives.

When she was twenty years old, St. Thérèse of Lisieux wrote a letter to her sister Celine, who was experiencing a difficult moment and lacked confidence. In this letter, St. Thérèse described a little child alone on a lost boat in the sea. The child may or may not know whether it is close or far from port. When contemplating the coast, the child perceives the distance made and how far the boat has gone. Seeing that the shore is further away elicits joy in the child's heart. But the more distant the shore, the more immense the ocean appears. The child's knowledge is reduced to nothingness. St. Thérèse wrote the word "KNOWLEDGE" with capital letters. The knowledge of the child is reduced to nothingness. It does not know where the boat is going. Since the child does not know how to steer the boat, the only thing that it can do is to surrender itself. It can let the boat sail in accord with the wind. You, like the child, are not alone in the boat. The captain is there. Jesus is present, but He is asleep, as once on the fisherman's boat in Galilee.

This imagery describes the exercise of the theological virtue of hope. The theological virtues have God as their object, and they are derived from God. Their motive is God, and so they touch God. We need to introduce the practice of the theological virtue of hope into our lives; this puts us into the hands of God.

We will find out our vocation at the moment of death. We live from day to day, trusting that we are in the hands of God, accepting that we are led in a mysterious way. What is the most important moment of our life? What is the moment at which we have given the most? We will find out at the moment of death. God does not give us our vocation as we enter a seminary or just before marriage. God will inform us of our vocation at the moment of death. Meanwhile, we live out hope day by day.

Great things are born in the Church through the power of God, not by our own success. Indeed, purification entails not only liberation from evil projects but also from the good ones that are our own and that we cling to. Of course, we need to have projects.

We need to have great desires. We need to want to do great things while at the same time being childlike before God. We do not impose upon God that things must be done our way, as did the two brothers in the parable. We must not cling to our projects, demanding that God make them happen. God always messes up our projects and leads us in ways that we never expect. We need to plan, and we need to strive for the good but in a humble openness to God without imposing upon Him our plans.

A do-gooder is proud. A Christian trusts in God and is generous in his response to what God is asking him. That is why good projects, even those suggested by God, pass through difficult phases and crosses that liberate us from attributing success to ourselves. The divine pedagogy, the way that God leads us, allows for crises in our personal lives. This often happens in marriage and in a religious vocation. At the beginning of a marriage, the couple is infatuated with each another; they fall in love, they get married, everything is wonderful. Four or five years after the wedding, they are tired of each other's jokes, and they are fed up with one another. Suddenly, a crisis comes.

Alternatively, after a priest has spent six years in the seminary studying, he is ordained; he is joyful, he goes to his parish, he has something to say while preaching, he remembers the notes of his classes, and so on. Five years later, he starts to think about money. He had never thought about money. He thinks about becoming a monsignor. Suddenly, he has sexual temptations which he never really had in the seminary. This is normal.

As God leads us, and as we try to live with God, we still have our weaknesses, and we still commit sins. We find a way to peacefully coexist with things within us that are not really of God. God accepts that—for a moment, sometimes for several years. Then suddenly comes the crunch, the crisis. A crisis is the moment when you realize you cannot continue living as you did. Either you make a deeper step toward God, or you crash. You recognize that a marriage is between a man, a woman, and God, and you trust in the power of the graces of the Sacrament of Matrimony. Up until then, you had not really thought about it, because everything was fine. Crises force us to either lean deeper into God and to trust His grace, basing ourselves upon it, or else do something stupid such that our lives crash. The same in the priesthood. The priest ultimately has to believe in the power of the graces of the priesthood and not on his own brilliance, wit, charm, and so on. God allows for crises, which force a change in our personal lives.

This happens also in religious communities, which periodically go through a period of crisis, and also in the lives of local churches. After the Second Vatican Council, the greatest crisis hit those local churches which were most proud. Some claim that Vatican II was the Council of Louvain celebrated in Rome, because the influence of theologians from the University in Louvain, Belgium, was so great. The Belgians, Dutch, Germans, and French were the most influential at Vatican II. After the Council, the greatest crises hit Holland, Belgium, Germany, and France. God allows these crises to come when the Church is too proud. I think Poland is falling into a crisis now, which will force an inner conversion. In the universal Church, about every four hundred years, there is a major crisis—the Eastern Schism, the Reformation... maybe now we are at the next stage?

A crisis places us in a situation where we cannot continue as before. We have to base ourselves on the love of divine charity, which is infused within us. We should not react like the unwise theologians who were the friends of the biblical Job. Job was a rich man with a big family and lots of property. Suddenly, he was hit by sickness; his children were killed, and he lost all his riches. His friends told him that it was his fault because was a sinner, but Job protested. There was no major sin that could have caused this. It was God who caused the crisis, using the devil.

The same thing happens in religious communities. Some religious communities of sisters have crashed, and the few survivors blame them because they changed the habit or reduced the length of the veil or dropped it all together. Those who changed things tried to be faithful to God, to their superiors, and to changes which came after Vatican II. Yet the crisis came. Those who were unfaithful left. But those who stayed were faithful. Yet the crisis came, and now many religious orders are dying out. We should not place blame on decisions around certain details. God, in His divine pedagogy, generates crises which force a deeper openness to God, a deeper conversion.

How is hope deepened? St. John of the Cross follows the thought of St. Augustine. Augustine tied hope with memory and with the paternity of God. Augustine had a pleasant little framework—the will, the reason, and the memory; the Father, the Son, and the Holy Spirit; and faith, hope, and charity. He attached all three so he had nine elements all tied together. Aquinas disagreed, because memory is not a spiritual power. Animals also have memory. Elephants never forget. Accordingly, the elevation of memory to the rank of a spiritual power of equal level as the reason and the will is sort of forcing the psychology to make it fit into a pleasant little schema. But there *is* an intuition in this. St. John of the Cross noted that we grow in hope through the purification of the memory because we can be attached to memories, both good and bad, and make an idol of our memories. This attachment prevents us from opening up to the divine mystery unfolding in our lives.

Sometimes, a mother has had a wonderful family with children and husband all around the table. She was happy. She was running a family. Then the children grew up. Some boy came and took her daughter. Some unpleasant woman came and took her son. Now, the mother is a grandmother and a mother-in-law. She protests that someone took her daughter away or that someone else is cooking for her son. The mother-in-law has good memories of the time when she was running the show. But now, she must adapt to a new stage in life and let go.

A priest was a pastor in a parish. Everything was great. He baptized the babies, catechized the people, built the church, and so on. Suddenly, the bishop sends a young priest, but he pushes back and says that it is *his* parish since he built it and knows everybody in it. But it is *not* his parish; it is God's parish. He has to let go. We grow in hope as we let go of attachments.

Also, bad memories have to be dropped. This is a problem that sometimes Jews have, as they do not believe in the Redemption. That is why they are hooked on their bad memories. They are constantly talking and thinking about their suffering. They want everybody to think about it and talk about it. They cannot let go, because they do not believe that suffering was redeemed by Christ.

When Pope Benedict XVI came to Auschwitz, there was a meeting with a group of people who were imprisoned there during the Second World War. They were children at the time. Those who were adults had long died. The pope met with them, and I watched on Polish television an interview with two ladies, one who was obviously Jewish and the other a Christian. The Jewish lady said, "It was horrible, it was terrible—we were children, we were in panic, we were in fear, we were hungry, we were beaten—it was brutal, It was horrible. And my life has been ruined. I'm constantly thinking about this and dreaming about this. My life has been a total wreck as a result. I constantly need psychic help to get me out of this." In the interview with the other woman, she recounted, "It was horrible, it was terrible—we were afraid, we were hungry, we were beaten. But then the war ended, and I had sixty years of a happy life." One let go of the suffering, and the other was hooked on the abuses that she suffered—true abuses—but without the capacity of letting go.

Hope is formed when we let go of the attachment to memories, whether good or bad. It is then that we can accept that we are being led to something new. The purification of hope also includes a social dimension. The disciples on the way to Emmaus had a political hope. It had to be shattered and purified by the Pascal mystery. We are tempted to think of success in a temporal sense, for example, the triumphalism of the Church. We live in time, and we live out charity in time. But hope leads us beyond time to eternity. In contrast, ideologies are shortsighted, expecting immediate, visible success. The revolutionary with his ideology must see success in his lifetime. In contrast, the Church knows that we need to pass through the Cross. Perhaps the fruits of the suffering which one is living out in hope and the love of God will come after one's death.

In the twelfth century in southern Italy, there was an abbot named Joachim de Fiore who proposed a theory that there are three stages of history (by the way, some of his views on the Trinity were condemned by the Fourth Lateran Council). The first stage belonged to the Father and the laity during the time of the Old Testament. Then there was a second stage of history which belongs to the Son and to the clergy, calculated to end around the year 1270. Finally, he expected a third stage of the Spirit with spiritual men. These ideas had a great influence in the thirteenth century, and the Franciscans were a bit tainted by this. In fact, the general of the Franciscans was deposed and imprisoned for this view. He was replaced by St. Bonaventure, who then wrote the official biography of St. Francis, deleting the apocalyptic expectations held by some Franciscans.

Aquinas very rarely used the word *stultissimum* (very stupid), but he referred to this theory as being most stupid. We are not expecting a new stage in the history of salvation. We already have received everything in Christ. So, dividing the Trinity into three historical stages is completely wrong. This erroneous theory implies that history is a historical, deterministic process, functioning on its own, where even God is subject to this process, and in a gnostic way, we can discover its secret and fit into it.

Cardinal de Lubac wrote a study on the heritage of Joachim de Fiore. He demonstrated that this idea lived on in European culture, in the modern ideologies of the French Revolution, Nazism, and communism. They all embraced the idea that there is a historical process and now we have reached the final stage. The Third Reich was to last for a thousand years. When I came to Poland to study, there were banners with slogans along the lines of "Communism demonstrates the way of humanity" and "If you join the Communist Party, you're on the front line of this movement which will lead to the bliss of eternal communism." They implied that communism was an automatic, objective, historical end of time. In this conception of history, human liberty was reduced. You can understand and embrace the process, but you cannot stop it.

Similar ideas have appeared in the Church. Some say that the Holy Spirit was asleep until Vatican II, and then He woke up. We are now introducing changes because we are moved by the Spirit. Others say that He was awake, but now He has gone to sleep. Well, these are all ideologies about adapting Christianity, making it relevant and effective, according to our own ideas. There is a streak of the old heresy of Marcionism, a heresy of antiquity which rejected the Old Testament because it was too brutal, too full of wars and sins and so on. Just the New Testament, please! There also is the heresy of Donatism, against which St. Augustine struggled, which claimed that a priest who is a sinner while celebrating the sacraments renders the sacraments invalid. The Church rejected this as well.

Common to these heresies is the hope for a pure, sinless, immaculate, crystalline Church without sin, without the Old Testament, without sinful priests. This is a false hope. We need the Old Testament, because it shows the working of God through sinful humanity, through wars, polygamy, and violence. Yet throughout it all, we see the hand of God. God is working through our lives, which are not ideal, and through our families and through our communities, which are not ideal. But we do not panic, because we trust God. Within history, there is sin, there is filth, there is failure, but the mercy of God is unfolding itself. We are not to have a merely human, temporal hope. We should not be idealistic about ourselves or our generation. We should not expect sin to end through some historical process. No.

There *is* an accumulation of knowledge over the centuries. We do not have to invent things which were invented before. So, yes, there is an accumulation of knowledge and a certain accumulation of wealth. But there is no accumulation of morality. Every generation is responsible for itself. Morality today may be lower or higher than in the past. New challenges and new issues appear. But every generation is responsible for its own culture.

The more important questions are: Do we trust God? Do we bring the power of grace through faith, hope, and charity into the world? God is pleading for our minds and hearts to bring divine love into the world where He has placed us. We should not be idealistic about ourselves. Nor should we embrace the idea of historical determinism, which claims that the historical process marches on regardless of our actions, denying personal liberty and personal responsibility. When we relate to God as trustful children, He operates in the world through our humble response in spite of, or even precisely due to, our weaknesses, which are offered to God for His purification.

Remain in My Love

"Remain in Me as I remain in you. Just as the branch cannot bear fruit on its own unless it remains on the vine, so neither can you unless you remain in Me. I am the vine, you are the branches. Whoever remains in Me and I in him will bear much fruit, because without Me you can do nothing. Anyone who does not remain in Me will be thrown out like a branch and wither. People will gather them and throw them into a fire, and they will be burned. As the Father loves Me, so I also love you. Remain in My love. If you keep My commandments, you will remain in My love just as I have kept My Father's commandments and remain in His love.

I have told you this so that My joy might be in you and your joy might be complete. This is My commandment: Love one another as I love you. No one has greater love than this. To lay down one's life for one's friends. You are My friends. If you do what I command you, I no longer call you slaves, because a slave does not know what his master is doing. I have called you friends because I have told you everything I have heard from My Father. It was not you who chose Me but I who chose you and appointed you to go and bear fruits that will remain, so that whatever you ask the Father in My name He may give you. This I command you. Love one another."

—John 15:4–17

During the Last Supper, Jesus taught the disciples about divine love. Just like the vine gathers sap from the root, so we are made capable of loving when we are tied with the Trinity through our faith in Jesus. Love is not just a commandment. It is a gift. We *receive* divine love, but we are *invited* to live it out. We know that the term love is often used and abused. It has many meanings in common parlance. So, to make things easier, the Church has a special word — charity — to describe supernatural love.

Unfortunately, some languages — like Polish — do not have a special word for divine love. Preachers may speak about charity while thinking about divine love, but they still use the word *love* even if they add the adjective *divine*. Many, especially the young, understand by that word *emotional* love; it is the only love they seem to know. They think of divine love as an experience more intense than erotic love. This is the difficulty we have in Polish. But in English, we have the word *charity*, which has a specific meaning.

This divine supernatural love — charity — is infused in us by grace. We received this love in Baptism, but of course, it has to be developed. This "computer program" installed in us has to be unpacked. The basic, practical question is what is this love? How do we experience it if we do? How do we unpack it? How are we to live out this divine love in our lives which are conditioned by the circumstances of our life, our profession, our career, our vocation? Divine love is mysterious. It is a consequence of faith. So, first, we encounter God through the exercise of faith, triggering the supernatural life in us. In contemplative prayer, we exercise faith by believing in the supernatural quality of faith. Faith enables us to touch God. It leads our mind out toward the life-giving mystery. The regular practice of faith within our prayer habituates us to base ourselves upon that mystery.

Faith is followed by hope, which adapts the will to the divine mystery unfolding in our lives. In hope, we trust that we are in the hands of God, that God is in charge. God is wise; He knows where He is leading us. Faith and hope give us the courage to walk on water. We go forward in life, believing in Jesus. We learn how to base ourselves on that solid foundation, that is, we learn how to walk on water. Sometimes, it is easy such as when the lake is frozen. But we have to learn how to walk on water even when it is not easy, based on the divine mystery, the divine promises, and on a fraternal encounter with Jesus, through Whom we are led to the heavenly Father. This pilgrimage in faith and hope awakens us to the reality of divine love, which is a gift. A gift that is demanding, but nevertheless it always remains a gift. The fundamental approach on our part is to engage in a relationship with the living God, for which we have deep gratitude.

St. Thérèse of Lisieux wrote shortly before her death a text addressed to God:

> You know, my good God, that I have always desired only to love You. I have no other ambitions. No other glory that I am looking for. Your love has preceded me from my

childhood. It has grown with me, and now it is an abyss, the depth of which I cannot fathom. Love draws love. And so, my love, my Jesus, is reaching out toward You. It would like to fill the abyss which is attracting it, but alas, it's not even a drop of dew lost in the ocean. To love You as You love me, I have to borrow Your own love. And only then will I find repose. Oh, my Jesus, maybe it is an illusion, but it seems to me that You could not fill a soul with more love that You have filled mine. And so, I have the courage to ask You to love those that You have given me, as You have loved me.[1]

In these words, there is gratitude for supernatural love, which Thérèse did not receive because of any work on her part. This supernatural love has preceded her existence. It grew in her as she grew as a child, an adolescent, a young Carmelite sister. Divine supernatural love accompanied her and was infused in her soul before she was even aware of it. This supernatural love enabled her to love God and to live her days in friendship with God. She was aware of her limitations, even in how she received divine love. Divine love within her is incomparable to divine love itself. What she had of divine love within her is incomparable to the immensity of divine love itself. Since she was weak, a child before God, she surrendered to divine love, borrowing it so that she could use it to love God and to love others. And she used the words of Jesus from His prayer as the archpriest before the Passion. She courageously asked for divine love that would enable her to love others, particularly those who had been given to her, such as the sisters

[1] *The Story of a Soul*, Ch. XI, A Canticle of Love.

in her community in Lisieux, and those for whom she intercedes from Heaven, and hopefully, also for us.

This is the language of prayer. It is a simple language. It is experiential. It is easier for us to fathom this language than the language of theology, because it was written closer to our times. Thérèse did not engage in speculative theology. She is like a young girl sitting next to us who grabs us by the arm and exclaims, "Look! Look!" This doesn't mean that we do not need speculative theology, with its precise formulas, or the *Catechism*. Experiential descriptions touch us, while precise definitions provide clarity. In order to have convictions, to distinguish truth from error, and to live sensibly, we need something more than touching words. We need convictions to clarify things in our heads and allow us to make practical decisions. So, while having the experiential language of St. Thérèse, we can also look to the precise distinctions that we find in the theology of St. Thomas Aquinas.

What is this charity or this supernatural love which is infused in us? It is a love that is supernatural. It is not a product of our nature. It is the love that God has for us, that He infuses in our souls, enabling us to love God with a reciprocal love. It enables us to love other people with that same supernatural love. St. Paul says, "The love of God has been poured out into our hearts by the Holy Spirit who has been given us" (Romans 5:5). In supernatural love, we receive a life which has its own rhythm of growth. We do not necessarily perceive it, but it is there, and it is extremely resistant. It may seem to be absent for many years, but then suddenly it appears with full force, because supernatural love has life. It has its internal force of growth. It is a supernatural life, but it can grow.

What is this love? How does it function? What is essential in it? How can we open up to it? Why is it that we ignore it so often? Why is it that we can sometimes lock ourselves against it? These are extremely important questions, and maybe the most important questions in life. What are we to do when we perceive that human love is weak? What are we to do when purely natural, affective, erotic, willed love painfully shows its limitations? How can we grow in divine love? What can a married couple do when their natural, erotic, affective love at some stage dries up? Are they to divorce? Or can they base themselves on this supernatural love which has been promised them in the Sacrament of Matrimony? How do they open up to that? What are we to do in moments of crisis when our hearts have grown cold?

There are many descriptions of charity in the Word of God. Many aspects are shown: Love is kind, love is gentle, love is faithful. For example, we have the parable of the Good Samaritan or the wheat and weeds growing simultaneously. But what is it precisely? How does this supernatural love differ from purely natural love? Speculative theology tries to pinpoint the essential elements of supernatural love. Let us first look at common imprecise descriptions of supernatural love.

Some think that love consists in an experience, having affective, sensitive, erotic feelings. If this is how we understand divine love, then we are prone to search for intense gratification in prayer. We hope for enchanting or mystical feelings. Of course, religious feelings are stronger in youth than in old age, but their power is not essential in the love of God. You will not live out the love of God like a teenager all your life. An old person may lie in bed in pain and still love God and yet have no intense feelings that God is close. We need to persevere in prayer and in the love of God in darkness, in moments of sin, and in moments of pain.

Another attempt at defining love is to equate love with activity. This is the conviction of the do-gooders who are constantly generous, constantly doing something. This is a sort of Pelagianism, or what Pope Leo XIII called "Americanism," when one counts on one's own forces with little appreciation of contemplative prayer. When do-gooders—who are constantly active—die, priests pray, "May they rest in peace." But in fact, the priest is praying not for the dead person to rest in peace but rather that their friends and family finally rest in peace.

At the opposite end of the spectrum, some equate love with the renunciation of experiences, with a stoic escape from feelings, a distance from all experiences and other people. This supposedly is love.

With divine love, there *are* moments of experiences. There *are* moments of activism, of generosity. There *are* moments of renunciation in charity. But all these moments are not the *essence* of charity. So, what is charity? Aquinas says that the essence of charity is friendship with God. To be a friend of somebody, there has to be an equal level, a common end, and an inter-exchange in view of that common end. A side effect of this is happiness. First, there has to be an equal level. We cannot be friends with a good wine, with a horse, or with a car, because there has to be an equal level between them. Some people treat people effectively and things affectively. They treat people like instruments and their car as an object of love. It should be the other way around. We should treat things effectively and people affectively.

Between God (or angels) and humans, there can be friendship. But how is it that we can have friendship with God if there's a difference between God, Who is supernatural, and we, who are natural? Aristotle said that being a friend with God is impossible. He was right, because he didn't know about grace. We are raised by grace to the supernatural level, and as a result, a friendship between God and us is possible. The distance between God and us has been abolished by the fact that we are raised to the supernatural level. There is a common end, which is our eternal encounter and happiness in God. This is what God wants for us and what we want. In this way, there is a fellowship with God, an exchange.

St. Paul writes, "God is faithful who called us to a community with his son, Jesus Christ" (1 Corinthians 1:9). We become friends with God, entering into relationship with the Persons of the Trinity, and this generates a fellowship, a community that may be maintained. This fellowship is focused on the common good. Love does not mean looking into each other's eyes. Love means looking together in the same direction, so it has to be clear what the common good is. In supernatural love, the common good is the proper good of God. It is not the experience of the exchange which is at the center but rather the common good. There is a mutual benevolence in the love of a friendship, a concern for the true good of the other. In a friendship with God, this friendly exchange and concern for the other expresses itself through prayer, attentiveness to the promptings of the Holy Spirit, and reacting to these promptings freely.

In a friendship with the true Good, there may be occasional affective experiences. We may feel joy or a desire to serve or an impulse to renounce something. But at the center is the encounter with God. Charity, the love of God, continues when the possibility of service is diminished due to weakness or sickness, or when there is aridity and there are no emotional delights. The personal encounter with God is more important than the fulfillment of a certain portion of prayers. Of course, it is good to have a regular rhythm of prayer. But the extent of the prayers that we have, the way they are celebrated in our private life or in a community where we live, has to serve the development of charity.

We have to adapt, taking into account our life and its possibilities. Happiness is a consequence of true love. As we focus on the Other, God, reacting generously to God's suggestions, we experience happiness. This love between God and us in charity, which is supernatural love, flows out to people who are the friends of God. We love people with the same love as we love God. This love extends to people. If I have a friend, I also love the children of my friend. Now the children of my friend may be rowdy and difficult and noisy and sometimes enervating, but these are the children of my friend. I have a different relationship with them than to children in general, because they are the children of my friend. But if I am the friend of God, I am also the friend of the friends of God. Charity entails also loving those who are God's friends, either factually or those who are only potentially the friends of God. They have not yet engaged in a friendly relationship with God, but we can love our enemies, because potentially they can be the friends of God.

Charity entails loving those who are God's friends, actually or potentially. Thus, we can love our enemies, because our enemies are potential friends of God.

Charity is humane; even though it is essentially divine-infused, it passes through an authentic, mature, concerned personality reacting toward others. We do not love people with charity in a purely angelic way. We love people with our whole being, our whole heart, with our whole personality. Charitable love has to be preceded by faith and hope. We view the other person with the eyes of God. We see them at a deeper level through faith. This means that we focus not on the evil that we perceive in the other person. Even if that evil is immediately visible, we focus on the divine moment in the other because we want divine grace in the other to be developed.

We should not panic, because we are in the hands of God. But in loving the other, we desire that the other person be a saint. This is the essence of the unitive dimension of marriage: a mutual help on the way to Heaven. A mutual help in the pilgrimage to Heaven. But basically, this love means that I want you to be a better person. That's why it is good to encourage engaged couples to reflect: "Jack, has Jill, as a result of your love, become a better person or a worse person? And Jill, has Jack become a better man or a worse man as a result of your friendship?" I want you to be a better person.

We love our neighbor in view of God. It is not a question of loving God in others but loving the other in view of God. It is not only the spiritual dimension in the other person that I love, but I also perceive the neighbor's needs. If my neighbor is hungry, do I feed him? But I do this not only in view of finding some way of resolving social problems. While you feed him, you are concerned about his salvation. Charity is inscribed within human relationships that have their own natural dynamic and order. Thus, it is normal that some people are closer to each other than to others. This is not contrary to charity. The love of neighbor is preferential.

The idea that the love of neighbor should be equal toward all is erroneous. Unfortunately, in many places and for a long time, this idea was held that, for example, in a community of sisters, each has to love each other equally. But if you love everybody equally, you do not love anybody. No, love is preferential. Aquinas was aware of this thesis that all should be loved equally, and he reacted angrily against it, which was very rare for him. He said this is *irrationabiliter dicitur*—this is irrational, the claim that love has to be equal. No, love has to be preferential. There's nothing wrong in the fact that we love our family more than we love the poor in Syria, even though the poor in Syria may be in greater need than our own family. But they are more distant to us. There is an order of responsibility which is natural. It is an order of affinity, and divine love is inscribed in that order. We love our family and those who are close to us with greater love than those who are distant, even though those who are distant may have greater needs.

Now many wounds, particularly in modern religious life, resulted from the failure of understanding this principle. In antiquity and the Middle Ages, this was understood much better. We must not avoid preferential love. But of course, love has to be open. It cannot be possessive and exclusive, where I come into a room, and if my friend is not there, I walk out. No, the heart has to be open. But there is nothing wrong with entering a room and approaching friends with whom I am close instead of those with whom I am distant.

Even in marriage, mutual love opens up toward the love of children and the love of other people. The couple who truly loves one another can serve others well. The teacher or doctor who interacts with many people will find it very straining and difficult to love patients as a doctor or love children as a teacher if he truly loves nobody or if he does not have a family or if he is not loved in a family. We have to love some people at a deeper level to be able to love others. Expressions of love are differentiated, and expressions of love are constantly new. They are constantly new and creative. We are inventive. We find new ways of expressing our love.

Now charity, this infused love which we have from God, has an impact on all the other virtues. There is an influence, a diffusion of charity on our entire moral life. Aquinas makes a very important distinction here, which is extremely demanding. He expresses it in his scholastic language, but I'll explain what it means. He says charity has God not only as the ultimate end of action but also as the formal reason of action. He says acts may be made in view of God, but they are to be in view of God as a formal and not just a final cause. So, in them there is to be not only a general finality, because we are called to do everything for God, maintaining a conscious focus on God.

Let us say you offer someone a glass of water. This may be a gesture of altruism based on a natural perception: someone is thirsty, so I will offer a glass of water. Or it may be an act of the virtue of justice, a good moral act. Or it may be because I just want to empty the bottle because I have too much water, and I want to throw the bottle out. But there may *also* be a concern for the other person's sanctity. Aquinas says that for this act of giving a glass of water to be not only an act of justice but also an act of charity, it is important that God be not *only* the general finality—whereby I do everything out of hope of getting to Heaven or with the general view of God at the end of my life—but also formally by focusing on God in the very *act* of giving. In this way, the act of offering a glass of water becomes an occasion in which what is important is not only the quenching of another's thirst, but the true good of the other. And the true good of the other is his sanctity. I want you to be a better person; I want you to be closer to God. The fact that I offer you a glass of water because you are thirsty is only the occasion to express something much more serious and much more important—my concern for your sanctity.

This is extremely demanding. Of course, we cannot always consciously have this focus. But in our acts of generosity and in our contact with people, we must have this focus on something more than just the good functioning of the social order, be it the order in a particular family or in the broader social order. We should focus on something more because we are concerned that the other person also becomes a friend of God, living out that fellowship with God through our Brother, Jesus Christ, which is made possible in charity. I want you to be a better person and I am concerned if you become a worse person. That is why fraternal correction is the prime act of charity. This is because charity's primary focus is on God, and only then it moves toward others. When I perceive that someone is misbehaving, I react. Of course, it depends on the level of responsibility. We are responsible for our children. But when our children are adults, our responsibility is limited. Also with our friends, work colleagues, and so on, we may not always be able to say that we are concerned about their sanctity. But internally, we need to focus on something more than just on the purely social context and courtesy.

Aquinas says that we sometimes have to fraternally correct our superiors in religious life. But he says we have to do it *suaviter in modo, ne exasperentur*, in a delicate way, so as not to exasperate them. There is wisdom here based on experience. There is an order to charity. First, we are concerned about our own salvation, of getting to Heaven, our own friendship with God. Accordingly, we cannot commit sins for the benefit of a loved person, because we are concerned about our own sanctity. Then we are concerned about the other person's salvation, the other person's sanctity. Third, we are concerned about the material needs of others following an order of responsibility, which means that we are more responsible for our children, our own family members, our own country than for distant countries' needs. This concern for material needs also includes a responsibility for our own material needs. Thus, we need also to take care of ourselves, of our health, of our material needs, our future.

Love is a delicate little flower planted by God within us. Charity passes through our bodies, our emotions, our choices, our decisions. Sometimes, we make mistakes. Sometimes, infatuation takes over. But there is no reason to panic. If errors are made, they can be brought to the healing grace of God. That is why St. Paul says, "We are bold enough to approach God in complete confidence through our faith in Him, in Christ" (Ephesians 3:12). It happens sometimes that we make an idol out of somebody, and the idol becomes a screen that blocks out God. Well, if this happens, we need to return to the primacy of our focus on God. This does not mean the abolition of friendships, but their purification. We need to trust in the power of divine love, which has been given to us. As Thérèse said, "Your love has preceded me from my childhood. It has grown with me, and now it is an abyss, the depth of which I cannot fathom."

Supernatural Life
in Natural Life

"When I came to you brothers proclaiming the mystery of God, I did not come with sublimity of words or of wisdom. For I resolved to know nothing while I was with you except Jesus Christ and Him crucified. I came to you in weakness, in fear, and much trembling.

And my message and my proclamation were not with persuasive words of wisdom but with a demonstration of spirit and power so that your faith might rest not on human wisdom but on the power of God."

— 1 Corinthians 2:1–5

St. Paul was clear that he was gifted with a mysterious divine wisdom and power. The crucified Christ is the source of divine grace. And His total gift of Self is continued in the sacraments. As we believe, we have access to God; we can count on His wisdom and His power. Divine wisdom is greater than human wisdom, greater than Greek philosophy and all the sciences. Some translations of this text that I read speak not only about human wisdom but about philosophy, which is the love of wisdom. It seems that St. Paul knew the great philosophical tradition of the Greeks and insisted that here there is something more—the wisdom that God has imparted. This text refers not only to bizarre esoteric, sophist, ideological currents that have to be set aside. That's obvious. But also good human wisdom has to be dethroned; it is not the ultimate point of reference. This doesn't mean that there is no place for philosophy. Far from it. We need to use our minds. We need to trust in the natural power of our human reason. We need to liberate the mind from enslaving ideologies, skepticism, and from relativist confusion. We need to train the mind to perceive the truth and adhere to it. But here there is something more.

St. Thomas Aquinas, who was also a great philosopher, in his commentary on these lines of St. Paul, insists that philosophy is not to have the last word, because we base ourselves on the divine truth that we receive. But of course, faith provokes reason to go on. Pope John Paul II, in his encyclical *Fides et Ratio*, insists on going to the fullness of truth. Speaking about philosophy as a pastor, as a theologian, he provokes the reason to go on, not to stop, to go to the fullness of truth and not to be locked in skepticism. If we do not have confidence in the natural power of reason, how can we make decisions about our life? How can we resist temptations? How can we understand the world? But we have received something more. Human nature that we can study in philosophy, deciphering its inner logic, its finality, its sense, is encompassed in the eternal project of divine love. God chose us before the creation of the world and aimed at our filiation, our being a chosen child of the heavenly Father.

The gift of faith (for most of us) precedes our human understanding. Most of us were baptized before we started to think. The gift of faith goes further than the capacity of our reason; it reaches out toward the life-giving divine mystery. When we lie on our deathbeds and when all our human achievements and natural successes fade away, what will remain will be the loving hands of the eternal Father. It's important that the last human act that we do, namely dying, be an act of charity, an act of total trust and love of God. And of course, not only the last act but also our daily actions can be lived out in faith and charity. The power of the Holy Spirit, to which we have access when we exercise our faith, is to be used. That power is to be used in daily life. Those are the children of God who are moved by the Holy Spirit.

The apostles lived with Jesus. They heard His words. He breathed upon them and gave them His Spirit. They were witnesses of His Resurrection. Yet Jesus told them to wait in prayer for the descent of the Holy Spirit. There are as if various moments of the Holy Spirit touching us day by day in a deeper way. We received the Spirit at Baptism. We have been confirmed in the Spirit in the Sacrament of Confirmation. We receive the pardon of our sins in the Sacrament of Penance. We receive Jesus' food in the Eucharist. Yet we need to pray for a deeper infusion of the power of the Holy Spirit in our lives. Every moment of prayer, every retreat, is an occasion to strengthen our faith, to deepen our receptivity to the Holy Spirit, to become bolder in our acts of divine charity. Even though we have received the graces of Baptism, our perception of being touched by God is only intermittent on some occasions. As time goes by, we need to grow in a permanent relationship with God, trusting that we are in His hands, reacting to the promptings of the Holy Spirit, accepting that the power of God encompasses our entire being. This is a process in which there are surprising moments, periods of difficulty, periods of deeper conversion. This is normal, so we should not be surprised that there is a process.

St. John of the Cross puts forth the image of a piece of wood placed into a fire. Initially, there is a young, joyful flame around the piece of wood. But then the wood starts to crack, and heavy smoke comes out of the wood. Ultimately, it is transformed into fire. As we relate with God, initially there is a moment of joy—a joyful flame. A seminarian is happy, a young sister is delighted that she has entered the convent. Everything seems to be beautiful and joyful. But as time goes by, as we put ourselves in the presence of God in a repeated way, our weaknesses, our temptations, our uncontrolled tempers, our hidden disorders eventually come out. Sometimes, they come out during a moment of prayer, which seems distracting and strange. This is normal. Moments of crisis are normal. That which is not divine, when it is put into the fire of divine love, it comes out and appears in our imagination, in our mind before it is burned out. This is a step leading us to the moment when we are transformed into the fire of divine love. This is the spiritual life, the life of grace working within us. This is not something to be locked up in contemplative convents and monasteries. This is a gift of God which is to be lived out in all professions, in all vocations. We can bring down the power of God, like that woman in Capernaum who touched Jesus, and the power came out of Him. We can bring that power of God to our schools, offices, shops, homes, armies, our governments, and to the world in which we live.

In this process, in this mission, we need to hold onto the truths that speculative theology has perceived and clarified. Certain distinctions that I have been mentioning and certain realities must be clear. First, the conscience is an act of practical reason. With my reason, I perceive a challenge. It is not a question of feelings but of reason, which sees the truth of the matter. As I mentioned, the only negative woman in the Gospels, Herodias, saw the truth of the matter that her daughter was pleading for a father. Her conscience reacted well, but then her free choice, which followed her conscience, was awful and tragic because she rejected the light of the conscience in her. We need to train the mind to go toward the truth. We need to trust in the power of our conscience, the power of our mind to perceive the truth. It is not a question of feelings. People sometimes say, "Oh, my conscience made me do this." It is not their conscience but either their self-will or their fleeting emotions. Conscience is a question of reason, which sees the truth of the matter.

The virtues are stable capacities that coordinate the psychic forces, both the rational and the sensitive. Virtues coordinate our emotions, our reason and our will toward a perceived object. A virtue is more than an act. A virtue is a psychic reality. It allows us to respond to the true good that we have perceived with ease, speedily, pleasurable, creatively, using all our talents, all our possibilities, finances, technology, know-how, and our contacts to do the good. The infused virtues are a gift of grace. The infused theological virtues allow us to make contact with God. The infused moral virtues are also a gift of grace, but they need to be cultivated and developed. The acquired virtues are a fruit of natural effort, and they can arrive at only a certain level of moral honesty. The infused virtues add a certain note of playfulness to them. We do the good for the good pleasure of God, for His fun and His joy. They put us at His disposal. With our talents and our personal qualities, we can go for the true good shown to us by the Holy Spirit.

The primary virtues that we need to cultivate are the theological virtues: faith, hope, and charity. They are infused by God, and they have God as their object and motive. First, we need to establish contact with God by faith; we repeatedly need to make acts of faith, as our mind goes out beyond the limits of what the mind can control, toward the mystery. We touch God and are open to His force. Through hope, we accept that we are being led by God. As a result, we can express charity, which is love of God and also a love of others in view of God, loving people with that same love that we have received from God, borrowed from His heart.

The exercise of faith turns on the spiritual aerials, the gifts of the Holy Spirit. These divine antennae in the soul enable us to catch divine waves and to recognize the promptings of the Holy Spirit, which always come by way of counsel. As we react, our infused moral virtues grow, and we become creative in the good that we do, because it is good. Those are the children of God who are moved by the Holy Spirit, who catch the divine waves and react to them. The moral virtues, of course, are multiple. But for convenience, they are grouped around the four cardinal virtues: prudence, justice, fortitude, and temperance. These are stable capacities of reacting creatively in view of the perceived good. They, too, need to be cultivated. The various moral virtues concern both our private and social lives. They bring something of divine charity into the reality of our lives. God pleads for our minds, our hearts, our inventiveness, our generosity so that something of the love of God will appear in the here and now of our lives. Charity, this divine love that we can borrow and use in our life now, is the only reality of Heaven that we can experience here on earth. As we live out charity, we already have one leg in Heaven, because we are living out the inner life of God.

As life develops over the centuries in history, with cultural and technical changes, new virtues appear as we perceive new challenges and new values. There are people who are creative in their generosity as they react to the values that they perceive. Classical ethics based on Aristotle did not speak about the new virtues that we perceive today, for example, the virtues of solidarity, ecological awareness (putting garbage into its proper colored dustbin), or transparency (being honest in financial dealings). Apparently in the Italian language, the word *transparency* does not exist. Now there is a problem in the Vatican, so they have had to bring in the Anglo-Saxon approach to the Italian management. It is normal that new virtues appear, especially in fields where there is a great development and change, for example, in medicine. There are constantly new challenges and problems in bioethics. We can say the same about economics, politics, and social life. Our inventive, creative generosity, stimulated by divine charity, perceives various places where we can put our hands to work and come up with something new.

Aquinas says that he who avoids evil because of divine precept is not free. We can reverse this and say that he who does good because he was told to do so is also not free. In contrast, he who does the good because it is good is free; he is a living icon of God. Christ is the icon of the heavenly Father. The image of the invisible Father is painted within us by the Holy Spirit, and we become the icon of the Icon, that is Christ. God is painting it not externally, with external cosmetics applied to our face, but from within. Our face is painted from within by the quality of our spiritual life. Something of the divine beauty shines on our faces as we are generous, creative, virtuous, as we come up with new ideas and new ways of living out charity. This is all well and good, but what do we do when nothing comes out of our good intentions? How many times have we tried to improve, and little has come out of it? So often we want to see immediate results of our actions. If we live our charity, maybe the goodness will be perceived much later.

At the funeral of St. Thérèse Lisieux, there were eleven people. She was a charming sister; she died of tuberculosis. Some of her sisters were already in the convent, but a few neighbors, people who knew her, came to the funeral. Her sisters discovered that she had written her *Autobiographical Manuscripts*. They published them as *The Story of a Soul*. Soon the book was sold out. People wrote and sent money to the convent, asking for more copies. Her spiritual fecundity began *after* her death. That's why she is a Doctor of the Church, because there are many, many saints of the modern twentieth century who were nourished by her writings. The fruitfulness of her charity appeared only after her death, whereas sometimes we want to see the results immediately. But this is not important. The important thing is to trust in God, to count on His grace, and to try.

There is a text of St. Thérèse in which she responds to the complaints of a discouraged novice who did not seem to be improving. This novice entered the novitiate, and things continued to be just as bad as they were before. St. Thérèse provided an image of a mother who is at the top of a flight of stairs. Down on the ground floor, there is a little baby that can barely walk. The baby looks up to the mother, wanting to reach her by trying to mount the first step but without success and falling back. It tries again. Finally, the mother, moved by the child's insistence, comes down, takes the child in her arms, and brings the child upstairs. This is the image of the primacy of the theological virtues. The eye contact of the child with the mother is like our eye contact with God. We trust in the power of God, and then we raise our foot up toward the first step. Do not think that you will make it up to the top. But try, and leave the rest to God. This is the theology of the infused moral virtues. This is how we grow in them, first by exercising the theological virtues: faith, hope, and charity addressed to God. Then we raise our little foot and try. But we leave the fruits to God.

St. Thérèse had an apostolate, and so she gave us the theology of the apostolate, because she had a mission given to her by the Church. It was not a great mission; she was made the assistant formator of the younger sisters. She herself was very young at that time, but in the closed community of the Carmelite convent, she was chosen to take care of the younger sisters. This was a true mission that the Church gave her, an apostolic mission to three younger sisters. St. Thérèse was perplexed by this, and so she wrote that, not knowing what to do, she hid her face in the arms of Jesus. Looking toward the face of Jesus, hiding in His arms, she asked Him to fill her little hand with such nourishment that would be appropriate for the sisters. Here again, we have the theology of the apostolate. First, the theological virtues: eye contact with God, with Christ, asking Him to provide a nourishment that is appropriate for the sisters.

If you have problems with your teenage kids, look toward God. Ask God to provide such nourishment that is appropriate. Then express what you perceive or understand, counting on the power of God. You may say something that seems banal, but the power of God will work in your words.

The same goes for preaching. Of course, we need to prepare what we say. We cannot count on the Holy Spirit doing all the work. We need to prepare something. But as we preach, we count on the power of God to make these few words that we have prepared appropriate nourishment. Maybe they will help one person sitting somewhere at the back of the church. Perhaps fifteen years later, we meet someone who tells us, "Oh, Father, I remember when you preached. You said such and such." "I said that?" "Yes, you said that, and it was very important for me." This is the power of God working through our words. But this apostolate is not only in church from the pulpit. It is also in your families, your offices, among the people you meet. You may meet people with resistances against the Church, and you cannot preach full theological discourses to them. You may only say a few words, perhaps not even mentioning the name of God. But you can look toward God, count on His power, and say what you perceive to be appropriate and true. Do not expect an immediate reaction. But your words will be supported by the power of the Holy Spirit.

This is a program for the type of presence that God expects of us. We are to bring the supernatural life of grace to our workplace, our families and friends, and to all human contexts. By inviting God in an act of faith and performing little gestures of charity, which are true and authentic, we are changing the world from within. We are bringing a bit of Heaven to wherever we are. We are making human relationships more humane and more divine at the same time. To understand this, we refer to the metaphysical principle that the first cause can be present in the second cause in such a way that the second cause is not denied in its dignity, as it is moved by the first cause. In other words, God can work in our human world in such a way that God is not manipulating us. We are not enslaved by God. God is working within our will in such a way that our acts, what we do, are one hundred percent ours. At the same time, they are one hundred percent divine when they are preceded by faith centered upon Jesus. It is not a question of either/or, but simultaneously both. God is working through us, and so what we do is one hundred percent ours, and at the same time, it can be one hundred percent divine.

This is something that was forgotten at the end of the Middle Ages. Martin Luther looked upon his own frailty, and yet he believed in Christ. He viewed the divine cause in our acts as being either/or. He claimed therefore that human nature is corrupt, with nothing good in it, and so he directed his faith to Jesus. But he did not believe that Jesus can change something in us. He viewed the grace of Jesus as being uniquely external, as though we are covered by a curtain, by the merits of Jesus. But underneath that curtain, we remain as corrupt as we are. Luther did not accept the existence of the sacraments or of infused virtues being the working of grace within us. Because he held to his either/or thinking—either human nature or grace, and he chose grace. Centuries later, Karl Marx, again thinking that it is either/or, said "I want man." So, he had to get rid of God to build on man. Then came Nietzsche, who said, "Well, if there is a God, I can't imagine anybody else being God apart from me." Many are falling into this trap today, thinking that they are the center of the world. No. God can work within us if our acts are preceded by faith. We call upon the power of God, and then what we do, the little things that we do, are nourished by the grace of God working within us. Yet what we do is one hundred percent ours and one hundred percent divine at the same time.

The central moment of Catholic social ethics is not external but internal. It is not a question of struggling to ensure that the constitutions of our states, our laws, our liturgical ceremonies during the coronation of kings are Christian. What is more important is that the internal dispositions and acts of individuals be animated by charity, which generates creative moral virtues. The Church is present in the world through the personal gestures of individuals, through consciences that perceive the true good, and through the virtues that react to that perceived true good, stimulating good action. The structural concern of Catholic social ethics is such that there should be a place for grassroots initiatives led by people reacting to the true good that they perceive.

In the medieval Catholic perception of social ethics, public law had to respect private law. In medieval England, France, and Spain, the king respected the rights of individuals and of the gentry to have their structures or the clergy to have their structures. Religious orders had their constitutions, and guilds of craftsmen had their ways of functioning. Universities had their autonomy, and the king had to respect that. In medieval England, the king had no right to enter the cottage of a peasant without permission of the peasant. Try that in Russia. But this was the Catholic ethos: the state has to respect grassroots initiatives.

Europe also knew another model that continued until the end of the Middle Ages in Constantinople. The Byzantine Empire was based on the primacy of public law and the complete destruction of the private law. It was a centralized police state with heavy taxation. Whenever there was a crisis, there was more centralization, more power and wealth were concentrated in the capital, which was rich. In contrast, the peripheries were poor and deteriorating, while the Muslims advanced. There was a current within medieval Europe, one that was embraced by the Holy Roman emperors of the region now known as Germany. They set their eyes on Byzantium and dreamed of unifying Europe in a Holy Roman Empire. The wars between the emperor and the papacy were basically about this. Is the state to impose its power, or is there to be room for free initiatives?

As the German emperors invaded Italy throughout the Middle Ages, the Italian cities fought for their liberties, which meant the right to function according to their own rules, traditions, and organizing structures, even those of the various ethnic groups in the region, such as the Jews and gypsies. This applied to the clergy as well. Every group had the right to function according to its own system. After the German invasions, the liberty to function according to their own ways was abolished, and one had to obey the power of the emperor.

Europe also knows another model coming from Mongolia, which has formed Russia, and to some extent Ukraine and Belarus. Even Poland was partly influenced, and certainly Turkey. This is the Mongolian and Ottoman tradition but not the Byzantine tradition. Here there is only private law, the private law of only one individual—the tsar, khan, sultan, first secretary of the communist party, or the dictator. At the lower levels in the power structure, a ministry or local government, the heads behave like little tsars or dictators. This means absolute submission to those who are above and brutality toward those who are below.

When our brethren reopened a Dominican parish in St. Petersburg, Russia, there was a layman helping out in the church sacristy. He constantly wanted to kiss the hands of the priests; he was very submissive. Yet he was unpleasant toward the altar boys, such that he had to be dismissed. But he did not understand, because this is common in the Russian ethos. Just a few days ago, there was supposedly a coup in Turkey. But it seems that it was organized by the president in order to have an argument. Now immediately afterward, he demoted two thousand judges, university professors, and so on. He had a list already prepared which contained whom he wanted deposed. It was a fake coup to give him the power to become even more like the sultan. This is completely contrary to Catholic social ethics.

In contrast, you in America are happy to live following the medieval Catholic social ethos, which the Puritans brought from England to America. The Puritans were wrong on the level of ecclesiology and sacramentology, but they were fighting the monarchs who were following the model of the emperors in Europe. The Bourbons, the Stuarts, and the Hapsburgs all wanted the same centralization, but the Puritans were fighting this, as they did not believe in the divine rights of kings. They wanted the liberty of the local government, so they came to America, and that is why America has flourished.

Religious liberty is not only concerned about the freedom of worship, which is permitted in Europe today, or the freedom to have personal convictions, which is permitted even in China. Religious liberty is the liberty to live out your personal life and your social life in accord with the ethos that you uphold, and to have a space for social virtues and your creativity, not only in your private and family life but also in your social life. That is why the less there is government interference, the better. Because then, there is room for virtues, for charity, for free initiatives in all fields of life—in personal life, family life, economic life, business, cultural life, educational life, social life, and political life. The more you have various entities which are not controlled by the state, the less people are alone. There is a buffer between the individual and the state. Whereas when there are no such entities and everything is controlled by the state, people are then locked in solitude, overpowered by an omnipotent state. This is what we have in Europe now. At every moment of crisis, they are saying *more* Europe, *more* centralization, *more* power to the bureaucrats in Brussels. And the peripheries are crashing, and the Muslims are advancing.

Socialism is born of the idea that public law is more important than private law. Socialism denies the right to live according to one's ethos. Education is the monopoly of the state. By imposing a fatalistic, deterministic vision of history, supposedly leading to inevitable progress, passivism is generated in people and also an egoist sense of entitlement. Since the government has taken most of my money in taxes, I cannot do anything. So, I have the right to receive on every level—education, healthcare, grants, and so on. This sense of entitlement is basically egoistic. I have a right to receive, but I have no obligation to give. This leads to increased debts that have to be borne by future generations. It is grossly unfair and contrary to the fundamental principles of Catholic social ethics if the state dishes out money, spends enormously, responding to the sense of entitlement, and places the debt on the next generation. This is the consequence of abortion. If it is okay to kill the unborn, it is okay to burden with debt the few that are born today.

St. Paul formulated that, "Children are not expected to save up for their parents but parents for their children" (2 Corinthians 12:14). It is a normal view of Catholic social ethics that parents work hard to ensure that their children grow up in better economic conditions than the parents had in their childhood. In some parts of the world—for example, the Indians of South America before the arrival of the Spaniards, many African tribes, and the Aborigines in Australia—this was not the norm. No, they ate what was there, and they did not care about the children. They had to care for themselves. Now, the Catholic ethos is reversed. Money is spent, and the next generation is expected to pay. At least in America, there is a debate about this. Even some of your bishops are responding. In Europe? Absolute silence. Nobody discusses this issue. It is clear for St. Paul. Children are not expected to save up for the parents but the parents for the children.

The more there is space for social virtues, for creativity, for response to divine charity, the better. The more there is breathing space and the more people are not alone, then there is a buffer between the individual and the state. If there is a net of relationships, of friends involved in the local schools, in local governments, in various NGOs, in various activities for good, the better. This is not because somebody told you that you have to do this but because you think it is worth doing.

Nonetheless, some virtues are still difficult. Why are some virtues so difficult? How can we explain the problem of addiction to drugs, alcohol, or sex? People are addicted, and there are some who are addicted yet they want to be free, and so they pray. Yet they fall. Just as there are societies that just do not seem to see what is obvious. They live according to a different ethos. In India, people live according to the caste system. Whether they are of the highest caste or of the lowest caste, if they believe this is how things have to function, they will never get out of it. In Islam, there is no place for personalism. Among the Australian Aborigines, there was never any concern for education. Gypsies also have little care for education. Even though we speak about natural law and try to perceive and understand the metaphysics of our being and its finality, many do not get it. Instinctively, they have a perception which is not in accord with the natural law.

The Western World, particularly after 1968 and the sexual and cultural revolution, has been plagued by deep confusion. Toward the end of the ancient Roman Empire, there was a poet who wrote about the *magnum delirium*, the great confusion. Basic values are unknown; there is moral relativism and chaos. As long as the economy functions, there is peace. But when someone has not formed a family or was never generous toward his children or was gay and spent money on pleasure, when the economy crashes, he will have no money, and the healthcare system may vanish. Then he will be lying under the bridge, begging. If you have no family to fall back on, no social networks, there is utter solitude and despair.

It is important that there will be the exercise of the virtues. But this requires a perception of the truth of the matter. And this perception of the truth of the matter is not only theoretical but also practical. It is the same reason that sometimes thinks theoretically and publishes books. But in practical action, we have to react immediately. This practical grasping of the truth is conditioned also by our sensitive cognition that is analogous to the sensitive cognition of animals. Animals have a sensitive cognition of what is good. What is good food, what is useful to build a nest, and so on. As we learn a language or a sport, we react immediately because in our brains there is a network that causes our body to react in a particular way. This movement in the brain is also conditioned by our environment and by our culture. That is how we pick up a language and how, when playing ping-pong, we do not theoretically reflect on the velocity of the ball before hitting it. We react immediately.

An animal may be trained to react in a way that is unnatural to it. But it becomes connatural to this particular animal. That is why such an animal may have a career in the circus, because it is deformed and it reacts in an unnatural way, which has become connatural to it. This is because the animal was deformed by a human being. That is why we find circuses interesting and pleasing.

There are also people who are deformed by the accumulation of their personal sins or by external environmental influences. They pursue something that is contrary to the natural law, something that is unnatural. But for them, it appears as connatural. Such connatural, instinctive reactions that are unnatural inhibit virtue. This is not new teaching. Aquinas knew about it, and he quoted a text attributed to Aristotle. Aquinas provided the example of people who have a connatural inclination to acts that are unnatural, giving a list of such actions: people who find pleasure in eating coal or eating soil or who find pleasure in homosexual acts, in sexual contacts with animals, and in cannibalism. These are examples of actions that Aquinas gave which are obviously unnatural and contrary to the natural law. Yet for some individuals, they seem to be connatural. Sometimes people say, "You Catholics always talk about homosexuality and the natural law, but my nature is different." There is a kernel of truth in this. Of course, his nature is *not* different; such an inclination is a deformation. But that deformation causes a connatural instinctive inclination toward that which is unnatural, which does not give internal peace and happiness, but in that individual it is instinctive. This makes growth in virtue extremely difficult. We see the consequences of an erroneous instinctive assessment of sexuality making chastity very difficult.

In Pope Paul VI's encyclical *Humanae Vitae*, section 12, there is a line which is badly translated. In all the languages that I know and in all the translations that I looked at, the pope spoke about the unitive and the procreative significances of the marital act. Then there is a line which is incorrectly translated. I approached the seven Latinists of the Secretariate of State who translate encyclicals into Latin (they speak Latin among themselves), and I said, "This is an erroneous translation." They insisted that it is correct, but I disagreed. Finally, they said: "There's a comma here that is unnecessary." Then I said: "If Paul VI put the comma there"—he was very attentive in what he said and wrote—"then it is important to take into account." "Ah, well, yes, if we take the comma into account," they agreed. As a result of the elimination of this comma, the reading of this encyclical became weakened. Paul VI wrote: *Etenim propter intimam suam rationem, coniugii actus, dum maritum et uxorem artissimo sociat vinculo, eos idoneos etiam facit ad novam vitam gignendam, secundum leges in ipsa viri et mulieris natura inscriptas.*

Janet Smith, who is a good writer, translates it this way: "Therefore, because of its intrinsic nature, the conjugal act which unites husband and wife with the closest of bonds, also makes them capable of bringing forth new life, according to the laws written into their very natures as male and female." This is obviously not true. The conjugal act does not make the couple *idoneos*, capable of receiving new life. Abortion, abandoned single mothers, parental egoism, violence, and abuse between sexual partners show that this is not true. This line should be translated as:

> Due to the intrinsic nature of the nexus of the two significances (of the bond between the two significances, the unitive and the procreative), which were mentioned in the previous sentence and are repeated in the following sentences, the marital act as it ties the husband and wife with a profound bond makes them apt to receive new life, according to the laws written into the natures of man and woman.

Only when both significances, the unitive and procreative, are mentally accepted and appreciated, can the couple grow in the virtues of parenthood. It does not mean that every act has to end in conception, but there has to be a positive appreciation of the possibility: "I love you, and I think you could be a great mom, and I want you to be the mom of our children." Or, "I love you, and I think you have the capacity to be a great dad. Well, not in everything, but I'll remind you about some details. But I want you to be the dad of our children, because I appreciate the value system that you express." Only when the unitive and the procreative are maintained mentally together are the married couple mature. The couple then grows in the virtues of parenthood, and then their mutual act can be an expression of charity. The Church is concerned that sexuality be lived out as a prime expression of divine charity.

There is a critique of the phrase "safe sex" in *Amoris Laetitia*. There is a line, "The concept of safe sex suggests the use of sex which is safe," meaning that it is defended against the enemy. Who is the enemy? The enemy is the child. The child which does not yet exist. It may not exist. But even though it may not exist, it already is treated as an enemy. God chose us before the creation of the world to be His adopted children, and here there is a "no, no, no!" The child is treated as an enemy, because the child demands parental virtues. The exclusion of the procreative dimension frees one from the obligation of growing in parental responsibility.

Chemical contraceptives poison the body of the woman. All contraceptives poison the soul of the man, who no longer has to grow in the virtues of fatherhood. If a woman says, "I want you, but I do not want you to be a father. I do not want you to grow in paternal virtues. I do not want you to be responsible. I do not want you to mature in responsibility," then he does not mature. He becomes an egoist and uses his wife as an object of his pleasure; then there are abuses.

The code of canon law speaks about marriage and about the good of the spouses. The good of the spouses is not some private need of the spouses against children. In the critical edition of the code of canon law, there is a reference to the sources, and at this point there is a reference to the encyclical of Pope Pius XI, *Casti Connubii* (which, incidentally, was the only preparation for marriage that my parents had—when they were engaged, they heard the encyclical read aloud in the cathedral, and that was all). But in that encyclical, Pius XI said that the unitive dimension consists in the concern for one another in the pilgrimage toward sanctity. The unitive significance is not just egoist pleasure, the experience of sensitive pleasure, but the mutual support to grow in charity and sanctity. When openness to charity and an appreciation of the value of procreation are maintained in the mind (that is, both significances tied mentally together), then the instinctive perception of the meaning of sexuality is correct and in accord with the nature of sexuality. Then the virtue of chastity is simple, almost automatic. Whereas when the appreciation of procreation is mentally excluded and only the mere sensitive union is focused upon, then chastity becomes extremely difficult. The focus on pleasure becomes an idol, which demands immediate and repeated gratification.

This distinction is important not only for laypeople but also for us celibates. Because we as celibates often think, "Well, procreation is not for me," we can fall into the trap of the contraceptive mentality, thinking that procreation is a "no-no" because I am celibate. Then maybe the danger arises of focusing only on the moment of gratification. Only when procreation is appreciated can the sexual force be handled and integrated into expressions that are chaste and respectful. When I, as a priest, see a young woman who is attractive, and I see this with my male eyes, I can say to myself: "Hey, she could be a wonderful wife and a wonderful mother. I hope she finds a great husband and has a good family." Then immediately, my reaction is chaste. But when, as a result of the contraceptive culture, the sexual dimension is instinctively perceived: "Ah, here is an object, a source of pleasure to me. But with the exclusion of procreation, because I'm a priest." Then chastity becomes difficult. The exclusion of procreation and the treatment of it as a danger, as an enemy that has to be avoided, wounds men and makes egoists out of men. Then they fail to grow in paternal virtues. That is why today, "a good man is hard to come by."

The same has to be said about the instinctive perception of the object of *social* virtues: the socialist sense of entitlement—"I have a right to receive"—the failure to distinguish between justice and equality, the failure to notice the difference between natural rights and acquired rights, and pacifism, which is tied with fatalism since there is an ongoing process that I can do nothing about. These reactions function not only on the rational level but also on instinctive perception, on the sensitive level. And this prevents growth in the social virtues. Openness to God and faith in charity, as they are exercised, lead to docility to the Holy Spirit. His inspirations are healing, but they are also demanding. The more we react to the Holy Spirit, the more profound are the suggestions that come from Him. And His power is purifying us. Those are the children of God who are led by the Holy Spirit.

Being Poor and Pure in the Face of God

"Someone in the crowd said to Jesus, 'Teacher, tell my brother to share the inheritance with me.' He replied to him, 'Friend, who appointed Me as your judge and arbitrator?' Then He said to the crowd, 'Take care to guard against all greed. For although one may be rich, one's life does not consist of possessions.' Then He told them a parable: "There was a rich man whose land produced a bountiful harvest. He asked himself, "What shall I do? For I do not have space to store my harvest."

And he said, "This is what I shall do. I shall tear down my barns and build larger ones. There I shall store all my grain and other goods, and I shall say to myself, 'Now as for you, you have so many good things stored up for many years. Rest, eat and be merry.'" But God said to him, "You fool. This night your life will be demanded of you. And the things you have prepared, to whom will they belong?" Thus will it be for all who store up treasure for themselves but are not rich in what matters to God."

— Luke 12:13–21

Blessed are the poor in Spirit, for theirs is the Kingdom of Heaven. Some people suggest that this should be translated: Blessed are those who have the heart of the poor man, for theirs is the Kingdom of Heaven. We are all in need, and we need to be beggars before God. St. Catherine of Siena said that we are all in a situation of need and we are all in a situation where we can give something. We need to ask others for various things, and we can also give. Had there been equality such that we would have all the same talents, all the same possibilities, the same possessions, where nobody would be in need and nobody would be in a position to give, there would be no charity. And so, God has arranged things so that the poor are with us always. All of us in some way are poor, not just financially, but poor in respect to God. We beg for His grace. St. Thérèse of Lisieux said that we cannot store graces. We cannot hoard them. We cannot say, "Hey, wonderful retreat. Now, I've got the graces. I'll hold onto them." No, the graces are given for the moment. The graces that you need tomorrow will be given tomorrow. And tomorrow again, you will be a beggar before God, pleading for His graces. Toward God, we are in a permanent dependence, in a constant situation of need, knowing that God is kind, that God is a Father, that God is willing to give us His graces. He gave us His Son Who took upon Himself the consequence of our sins and gave us the Spirit flowing from His open heart. We can always receive from God, but we must orient ourselves toward God with a pure faith and a pure heart.

Being transparent to grace and having a pure heart toward God means that we do not impose upon God our own projects. We are to accept the project of God. In the New Testament, we have various terms which are applied to Jesus. He is the Son of Man. He is the Son. He is the Word. He is the Gate. He is the Good Shepherd. But the two most important terms are "Son" and "Word" — *Logos* (Greek). The Word which became Flesh. St. Thomas Aquinas reflected for a long time, wondering what does this mean. He arrived at the conclusion that when we are thinking about something, sometimes we have the funny feeling that we have an idea at the tip of our tongue, but we cannot find the word for it. I sometimes find that I have a word in Polish, but I cannot find the word in English. Or I have the word in English, and I cannot find the word in Polish. Sometimes, we cannot find the word in any language, but we have some faint idea. Then there comes a moment when something clicks, when we can put a word or a name on the idea. This is a mental word.

Now the Word that became Flesh is the Word of God, the concept that clicked in the mind of God. God's plan for us became flesh, became Jesus Christ. In Him, we have the absolute truth. We have the Word of God for us, and we need to receive that mental concept in our own mind. Unfortunately, sometimes we erect mental contraceptives — ideas which block the divine Word, kill the divine love and its fruitfulness in us, and prevent the divine idea from flourishing in our lives. That's why we need to have a pure heart, a pure faith, a pure spirit, without erecting anything.

Holding onto our own ideologies means that we want to impose upon God our own ideas; we want to use God, manipulating Him for ourselves.

St. Maximilian Kolbe, the priest who was killed in Auschwitz, had a great devotion to Our Lady. All his life, he wondered about the relationship between Mary and the Holy Spirit. In the final text he wrote before he was arrested and sent to Auschwitz, he finally came up with an answer. He wrote that the Immaculate Conception is the proper name of the Holy Spirit, because the Holy Spirit is the One Who is absolutely open to the Father and the Son. He proceeds from the Father and the Son, and so the Holy Spirit conceives life into the world in an immaculate way. He does not impose upon the Father and the Son His own projects. He is completely transparent to the Father and the Son. We can therefore apply the term "Immaculate Conception" to the workings of the Holy Spirit.

Mary in her life of faith is most pure, most receptive with the movements of the Holy Spirit. But we, too, can in our lives try to live out pure faith without erecting obstacles, without erecting these mental contraceptives that exclude the project of God. The more our faith is pure, the more we perceive the idea of God and the promptings of the Holy Spirit for us in our daily life, day to day, the more our faith is pure—the more we can live out the truth that those are the children of God who are led by the Holy Spirit.